PERSUASION

▼

A Language Arts Unit
for High-Ability Learners

Grades 5–7

The College of William and Mary
School of Education
Center for Gifted Education
Williamsburg, VA 23187-8795

PERSUASION

A Language Arts Unit for High-Ability Learners

Grades 5–7

The College of William and Mary
School of Education
Center for Gifted Education
Williamsburg, VA 23187-8795

Center for Gifted Education Staff:
Project Director: Dr. Joyce VanTassel-Baska
Project Manager: Dana T. Johnson
Project Consultants: Linda Neal Boyce, Chwee Quek, Claire Hughes, Catherine A. Little

Teacher Developer:
Sandra Coleman

Grammar Packet:
Michael Clay Thompson

*Funded by the Jacob K. Javits Program, United States Department of Education,
under a subcontract from the Washington-Saratoga-Warren-Hamilton-Essex BOCES,
Saratoga Springs, New York.*

KENDALL/HUNT PUBLISHING COMPANY
4050 Westmark Drive   Dubuque, Iowa 52002

Cover image:
M.C. Escher "Three Worlds" © 1998 Cordon Art B.V. - Baarn - Holland. All rights reserved.

Contents

SECTION

I

UNIT INTRODUCTION AND CURRICULUM FRAMEWORK

This section provides the rationale for the unit and the core goals and student outcomes that frame its lessons. It also lists student reading selections, both core works and those used in extension assignments.

▼ Introduction to the Unit

This unit highlights persuasion, especially as it relates to oral communication. Emphasis is placed on providing evidence for opinions. Students must give passages from literature to defend their points of view in discussion as well as in written arguments. Opportunities are presented for impromptu speeches, informative and persuasive speeches, debate, small and large group discussion, and critical listening skills. Throughout the unit, students work on independent research on the topic of censorship and make an oral presentation of their opinions and supporting evidence at the end of the unit.

▼ Rationale and Purpose

Even though all four of the language arts strands are incorporated into this unit, the highlighted purpose of the unit is to enhance the oral communication skills of fifth through seventh grade high-ability students using literature and an emphasis on developing persuasive argument in speaking and writing. Activities are designed to develop the skills of persuasion in oral and written form. Oral communication activities include lessons which use discussion, drama, debate, and speeches. Students read and critique literature and learn to write persuasively.

The ability to conduct an effective verbal presentation is an important skill for persons of all ages and ability levels. Gifted students will often have many opportunities throughout their adult lives to make presentations to others. To enjoy the full range of communication available to them, they must develop their speaking and listening skills. Systematic instruction is necessary to ensure that students acquire appropriate skill levels in oral communication.

This unit focuses on skills which are important in oral communication. Skills of persuasion are developed through activities that require the student to learn to develop "proof" and identify best evidence and reasoning. These abilities are crucial for success in school and are linked to intellectual functioning and citizen participation in the working world.

▼ Goals and Outcomes

Content Goals and Outcomes

GOAL 1: To develop analytical and interpretive skills in literature.

Students will be able to . . .

    A. Describe what a selected literary passage means.

    B. Cite similarities and differences in meaning among selected works of literature.

    C. Make inferences based on information in given passages.

    D. Create a title for a reading selection and provide a rationale to justify it.

GOAL 2: To develop persuasive writing skills.

Students will be able to . . .

A. Develop a written persuasive essay (thesis statement, supporting reasons, and conclusion), given a topic.

B. Complete various pieces of writing using a three-phase revision process based on peer review, teacher feedback, and self-evaluation.

GOAL 3: To develop linguistic competency.

Students will be able to . . .

A. Analyze the form and function of words in a given context.

B. Develop vocabulary power commensurate with reading.

C. Apply standard English usage in written and oral contexts.

D. Evaluate effective use of words, sentences, and paragraphs in context.

GOAL 4: To develop listening/oral communication skills.

Students will be able to . . .

A. Discriminate between informative and persuasive messages.

B. Evaluate an oral persuasive message according to main idea and arguments cited to support it.

C. Develop skills of argument formulation.

D. Organize oral presentations, using elements of reasoning as the basis.

Process Goal and Outcomes

GOAL 5: To develop reasoning skills in the language arts.

Students will be able to . . .

A. Apply aspects of the Paul reasoning model through specific examples.

B. State a purpose for all modes of communication, their own as well as those of others.

C. Define a problem, given ill-structured, complex, or technical information.

D. Formulate multiple perspectives (at least two) on a given issue.

E. State assumptions behind a line of reasoning in oral or written form.

F. Apply linguistic and literary concepts appropriately.

G. Provide evidence and data to support a claim, issue, or thesis statement.

H. Make inferences, based on evidence.

I. Identify implications for policy development or enactment based on the available data.

Concept Goal and Outcomes

GOAL 6: To understand the concept of change in the language arts.*

Students will be able to . . .

- A. Understand that change is pervasive.
- B. Illustrate the variability of change based on time.
- C. Categorize types of change, given several examples.
- D. Interpret change as positive or negative in selected works.
- E. Identify elements of change in a piece of literature.
- F. Analyze social and individual change in a given piece of literature.

▼ Student Readings

Novels/Books	Author	Relevant Lesson
Journey to Topaz	Yoshiko Uchida	Lessons 1, 7, 23
Dragonwings	Laurence Yep	Lessons 1, 7, 23
The Secret of Gumbo Grove	Eleanora E. Tate	Lessons 1, 10, 23
Roll of Thunder, Hear My Cry	Mildred Taylor	Lessons 1, 10, 23
Going Home	Nicholasa Mohr	Lessons 1, 15, 23
Taking Sides	Gary Soto	Lessons 1, 15, 23
Morning Star, Black Sun: The Northern Cheyenne Indians and America's Energy Crisis	Brent Ashabranner	Lessons 1, 20, 23
Rising Voices: Writings of Young Native Americans	Arlene Hirschfelder & Beverly Singer	Lessons 1, 20, 23

Poems

"The Road Not Taken"	Robert Frost	Lessons 1, 3
"The Pied Piper of Hamelin"	Robert Browning	Lessons 12, 13
"Stopping by Woods on a Snowy Evening"	Robert Frost	Lesson 24

*See Appendix for a detailed discussion of the concept of change.

Book Chapters, Historical Documents, Essays, Speeches

from *The Adventures of Tom Sawyer*	Mark Twain	Lessons 4, 6
The Declaration of Independence	Thomas Jefferson	Lessons 9, 18
"Libraries Should Reflect Majority Values"	Phyllis Schlafly	Lesson 11
"Libraries Should Reflect Diverse Views"	American Library Association	Lesson 11
March on Washington Address ("I Have a Dream")	Martin Luther King, Jr.	Lesson 14
"The Case for Public Schools"	Horace Mann	Lesson 16
"The Velvet Hangover"	Václav Havel	Lesson 18

Play

The Valiant	Holworthy Hall & Robert Middlemass	Lesson 21

Extensions

"Birches"	Robert Frost	Lesson 1
"Putting in the Seed"	Robert Frost	Lesson 1
"After Apple Picking"	Robert Frost	Lesson 1
"The Gift Outright"	Robert Frost	Lesson 1
Peter Pan	J. M. Barrie	Lesson 12
Twelve Angry Men	Reginald Rose	Lesson 21

Additional Resource Literature

Beahm, G. (Ed.). (1993). *War of words: The censorship debate*. Kansas City, MO: Andrews and McMeel.

Public Agenda Foundation. (1987). *Freedom of speech: Where to draw the line*. Dayton, OH: Domestic Policy Association.

The New York Public Library. (1984). *Censorship: 500 years of conflict*. New York: Oxford University Press.

Censorship: For & against. (1971). New York: Hart.

Censorship: Opposing viewpoints. (1990). San Diego: Greenhaven.

Hirschberg, S. (1992). *One world, many cultures*. New York: Macmillan.

Miller, R. K. (1992). *The informed argument: A multidisciplinary reader and guide* (3rd. ed.). Fort Worth, TX: Harcourt Brace Jovanovich.

Ravitch, D. (1990). *The American reader: Words that moved a nation*. New York: HarperCollins.

SECTION

II

LESSON PLANS

The pages which follow provide some introductory information about the unit lessons, including a discussion of the alignment of lessons with unit goals, lists of key vocabulary words, and a letter to send home to parents about the unit. The unit lesson plans themselves appear after the parent letter.

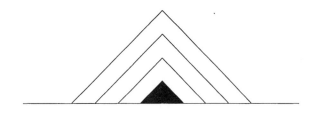

▼ Caveat for Teachers

The issue of book censorship plays an important role in the research component of this unit. The unit writers have tried to treat censorship as an example of a two-sided issue in which students are invited to argue their own point of view. However, teachers who use the unit should be aware that censorship revolves around issues of values, choices, and control. Some parents feel that these issues are inappropriate for the classroom. In addition, examples of censored materials may be brought to class during the research work of the unit, with the potential to generate real and unwelcome censorship battles.

This caveat is not intended to discourage use of the unit. We believe that censorship is an important issue that thoughtful, informed citizens should consider on a regular basis. We do, however, recommend that teachers anticipate possible consequences of the teaching of the unit and prepare accordingly.

▼ Alignment of Lessons with Unit Goals

The table below demonstrates which lessons contain activities specifically addressing each of the overall unit goals. Teachers should take time in each lesson to share with students how the activities relate to the overall goals and central theme of the unit.

GOAL	LESSONS
Goal 1: Literary analysis and interpretation	1, 3, 4, 7, 9, 10, 11, 12, 14, 15, 16, 18, 20, 21, 23, 24
Goal 2: Persuasive writing	1, 2, 5, 6, 8, 9, 11, 12, 13, 14, 16, 17, 18, 19, 20, 22, 23, 24
Goal 3: Linguistic competency	3, 4, 9, 12, 14, 16, 18, 21, 22
Goal 4: Oral communication	4, 6, 12, 13, 14, 16, 17, 18, 19, 20, 22
Goal 5: Reasoning	1, 4, 5, 6, 7, 8, 9, 10, 11, 12, 13, 14, 15, 16, 17, 18, 19, 20, 21, 22, 23, 24
Goal 6: Concept of change	1, 2, 4, 7, 9, 10, 12, 14, 15, 17, 18, 20, 21, 23, 24

Other emphases are also specifically addressed, as indicated in the following table:

EMPHASIS	LESSONS
Interdisciplinary Connections	6, 9, 12, 14, 16, 18, 19, 21
Student Research	11, 15, 20, 22

▼ Unit Vocabulary List

The list of words below contains suggested words for vocabulary study from each literature selection in the unit. The teaching model employed for vocabulary study is introduced in Lesson 3 and used throughout the unit; it is also described under "Teaching Models" in Section III.

Unit Focus:
persuasion

from "The Road Not Taken":
diverge

from *The Adventures of Tom Sawyer*:
circumstance
delectable
expeditions
melancholy
laborious
philosopher
ponderously
straitened

from the Declaration of Independence:
acquiesce
annihilation
consanguinity
despotism
jurisdiction
magnanimity
perfidy
rectitude
unalienable
usurpations

from "The Pied Piper of Hamelin":
consternation
mutinous
paunch
piebald
pottage

subterranean
vermin

from "I Have a Dream":
manacle
proclamation
redemptive
segregation

from "The Case for Public Schools":
factitious
feudalism
inestimable
prerogative

from "The Velvet Hangover":
august
catastrophe
paradox
totalitarian

from *The Valiant*:
autobiography
dubiously
felonious
indulgent
insouciant
malice
martyr
metropolitan
sovereign
vacuity
valiant

▼ Glossary of Literary Terms

The following list contains a selection of literary terms which may be useful for students to understand in the discussion of literature in the unit.

Character: a person portrayed in an artistic piece, such as a drama or novel

Climax: the turning point in a plot or dramatic action; a moment of great or culminating intensity in a narrative or drama, especially at the conclusion of a crisis

Denouement: the final resolution or clarification of a dramatic or narrative plot; the events following the climax of a drama or novel in which such a resolution or clarification takes place

Motivation: an inducement or incentive to action; in a story, the psychological or social factors that drive character action

Plot: the plan of events or main story in a narrative or drama

Setting: the time, place, and circumstances in which a narrative, drama, or film takes place

Theme: an implicit or recurrent idea; a motif; a central idea that permeates a poem, short story, or novel

Dear Parents:

Your child is engaged in a special language arts unit called *Persuasion*. It is organized around the concept of change and designed specifically to meet the needs of high-ability students. The goals of the unit are as follows:

▼ To develop analytical and interpretive skills in literature.

▼ To develop persuasive writing skills.

▼ To develop linguistic competency.

▼ To develop listening/oral communication skills.

▼ To develop reasoning skills.

▼ To understand the concept of change.

In this language arts unit we will study the concept of change through many different types of activities. We will consider the many ways argument and persuasion can be used effectively to cause change. We will also read a wide variety of literature which will provide the context for looking at change and perhaps reveal argument and persuasion in surprising places. Discussion, debate, public speaking, and writing will provide opportunities to persuade an audience and to personally create a change in ideas, thinking, and perspective.

In class we will read and discuss short pieces of literature—poems, short stories, speeches, and essays. Everyone will keep a response journal to clarify thinking and to help prepare for written and oral assignments. As we read the literature, we will respond to it and think critically about it by analyzing ideas, vocabulary, and structure. Specifically, we will look for insight into the concept of change and how authors argue and persuade. In addition to discussion, we will write short pieces, debate issues, and deliver speeches.

This unit includes the following independent projects which will be completed at home:

▼ An independent reading and writing assignment on multicultural literature.

▼ An independent grammar packet.

▼ A research project on an issue surrounding book censorship.

▼ Various short writing pieces.

Although the independent projects will be completed outside of class, we will discuss them in class. There will be opportunities to work with the teacher and classmates on each project as the unit progresses. The time frame for these projects is summarized in the schedule on the next page.

LESSON NUMBER AND DATE ASSIGNED	DESCRIPTION OF ASSIGNMENT	LESSON NUMBER AND DUE DATE
Lesson 1 Date:	Independent Reading Assignment	Lesson 7, 10, 15, 20 (one book per lesson) Date:
Lesson 3 Date:	Grammar Self-Study Unit	Lesson 22 Date:
Lesson 6 Date:	Collection of Advertisements	Lesson 19 Date:

Lesson 9
Date:
	Persuasive Letter	Lesson 12
		  (revising)
		Date:
		
		Lesson 13
		  (editing)
		Date:

Lesson 11
Date:
	Research project on the issue of censorship	Lesson 20
		  (revising)
		Date:
		
		Lesson 22
		  (presentation)
		Date:

Lesson 13 Date:	Debate	Lesson 17 Date:

The unit will be assessed in several ways. First, a pre-assessment will assess entering skills in the language arts areas of literature, writing, and linguistic competency. Secondly, a writing portfolio will document progress in writing. We will assess each project with a self assessment, a peer assessment, and a teacher assessment. Post-assessments will be given to assess exit skills in the language arts areas above. Finally, I welcome comments and feedback from you as parents.

Good curriculum and instructional practice should involve parents as well as teachers. The following ideas may be useful as your child experiences this unit:

1. Read the same books your child is reading and discuss the key ideas.
2. Research family history and heritage with your child.
3. Play games such as Scrabble® or Boggle® with the family to enhance vocabulary and language usage.
4. Encourage your child to every day in a diary or journal.
5. Try to set up a letter-arrangement with someone from another country or another part of the United States in order to encourage writing on a regular basis, either through regular or electronic mail.

6. When viewing film or television together, discuss the ideas presented with your child, and encourage close attention to how persuasion is handled in the media and how various cultural and ethnic groups are portrayed.

Thank you in advance for your interest in your child's curriculum. Please do not hesitate to contact me for further information as the unit progresses.

Sincerely,

LESSON
1
▼

Introduction and Pre-Assessment

CURRICULUM ALIGNMENT CODE

GOAL 1	GOAL 2	GOAL 3	GOAL 4	GOAL 5	GOAL 6
X	X			X	X

INSTRUCTIONAL PURPOSE

▼ To develop analytical and interpretive skills in literature.

▼ To administer pre-assessments for literature and persuasive writing.

MATERIALS USED

1. "The Road Not Taken" by Robert Frost

2. Pre-Assessment for Literature (Handout 1A)

3. Literature Interpretation Scoring Rubric for Pre- and Post-Assessments and Examples

4. Pre-Assessment for Writing (Handout 1B)

5. Persuasive Writing Scoring Rubric for Pre- and Post-Assessments and Examples

6. Independent Reading Assignment (Handouts 1C and 1D)

ACTIVITIES

1. Have the students silently read "The Road Not Taken" by Robert Frost and take the **Pre-Assessment for Literature** (Handout 1A).

2. Have students keep their papers and the poem to discuss the pre-assessment questions. Guide the discussion further with additional questions such as the following:

Literary Response and Interpretation Questions

▼ *How does Frost describe the two roads? What are the similarities and differences in them?*

17

- ▼ *What do the two roads in the poem symbolize or stand for? How are choices in life like the choice made in the poem?*

- ▼ *What do you think Frost means by the last two lines of the poem?*

Reasoning Questions

- ▼ *How does the speaker feel about each of the roads? Give evidence for your answer.*

- ▼ *What reasons could you give to support taking a "less traveled road" in life? What reasons could you give for taking a "well-worn path"?*

Change Question

- ▼ *This poem suggests that the choices we make determine the directions our lives take. Do you agree or disagree? How can choices change one's life?*

3. Collect the **Pre-Assessment for Literature**.

4. Distribute the **Pre-Assessment for Writing** (Handout 1B). Have students complete the pre-assessment, then discuss the question. After the discussion, collect the papers.

5. Ask students to recall a time when they had to make a decision that was like choosing between two roads (example: choosing between participating in two different activities whose schedules conflicted). Have them create a drawing which represents their choice as a decision between two roads. Invite them to illustrate the roads so that the picture explains more about the choice that was made, including such details as obstacles in the roads and the potential destinations.

6. Have students write a five-paragraph essay about their decision, using the drawing for support. The first paragraph should be an introduction to the essay, explaining the main theme of the piece. In the second paragraph, students should explain the decision that was made and the changes it created in their lives. The third paragraph should describe the road not taken and the changes it could have made. In the fourth paragraph, students should argue that one path was better than the other, explaining the factors that made the difference and whether they were pleased with the outcome. The final paragraph should provide a conclusion to the essay. Allow students to share their essays along with their drawings of the two roads.

7. Explain to students that during the course of this unit, they will be studying many types of changes, including the personal and social changes experienced within various cultural groups. As a part of this exploration of change, they will be reading selections which represent the Asian-American, African-American, Hispanic-American, and Native American cultures. Students will be asked to read selections and respond to them in writing, followed by class discussions.

8. Assign students to either Group A or Group B for the independent reading activities, and distribute to each group the appropriate **Independent Reading Assignment** (Handouts 1C and 1D). Discuss the assignment with students, and explain that they are to begin reading the Asian-American book on the list for discussion in Lesson 7.

NOTES TO TEACHER

1. *Please send home the letter to parents (see introduction to Section II) with each student who is engaged in the unit. Remember to sign the letter and to fill in tentative dates for assignment deadlines.*

2. *The pre-assessments in literature and persuasive writing serve multiple purposes. Performance on the pre-assessment should establish a baseline against which performance on the post-assessment may be compared. In addition, teachers may use information obtained from the pre-assessments to aid instructional planning as strengths and weaknesses of students become apparent. Rubrics are provided for the scoring of the pre- and post-assessments, followed by sample student responses with their scores.*

3. *The books for the independent reading assignment were chosen as examples of books that consider issues from a cultural or ethnic perspective. The titles for Group B (Handout 1D) are somewhat less complex than the titles in Group A (Handout 1C); teachers should assign students to the groups based on their understanding of various students' abilities and needs.*

HOMEWORK

Begin reading the Asian-American book on your list.

EXTENSIONS

1. Read "Birches," "Putting in the Seed," and "After Apple Picking" by Robert Frost. Make a chart comparing the three poems. List the pieces of the three poems that relate to the ideas of persuasion and change.

2. Read "The Gift Outright" by Robert Frost. This poem was read at the inauguration of President Kennedy; think about why it may have been appropriate for such an occasion. Give a two-minute speech to the class arguing for or against the choice of the poem for the inauguration.

3. Research the life of Robert Frost. Find out why people thought he was representative of rural areas, of the region in which he lived, and of the America of his time. Do you agree or disagree with this image? Give a speech to the class to defend your point of view.

Pre-Assessment for Literature

(Handout 1A)

NAME: _____ DATE: _____

Read the poem carefully and answer the questions below.

1. State an important idea of the poem in a sentence or two.

2. Use your own words to describe what you think the author means by the words, "I took the road less traveled by, And that has made all the difference."

3. What does the poem tell us about the idea of change? Support what you say with details from the poem.

4. Create a title for this poem. Give two reasons from the poem for your new title.

Literature Interpretation Scoring Rubric for Pre- and Post-Assessments

1. **State an important idea of the reading in a sentence or two.**

Score	Description of Response
1	limited, vague, inaccurate, confusing, only quotes from reading
2	simplistic, literal statement; uses only part of main idea; creates title rather than main idea
3	insightful, addresses theme

2. **Use your own words to describe what you think the author means by . . .**

Score	Description of Response
1	limited, vague, inaccurate; rewording only
2	accurate but literal response
3	insightful, interpretive response

3. **What does the poem tell us about the idea of change? Support what you say with details from the poem.**

Score	Description of Response
1	limited, vague, inaccurate; only quotes from story
2	valid generalization without support **or** well-supported example
3	valid generalization about change is made and well supported

4. **Create a title for this poem. Give two reasons from the poem for your new title.**

Score	Description of Response
1	limited, vague, or title given without reasons
2	appropriate but literal response; at least one reason given
3	insightful, meaningful title given with support

Sample Student Responses
Pre-Assessment for Literature

1. **State an important idea of the reading in a sentence or two.**

   SAMPLE 1-POINT RESPONSE:

   • *It's about wandering down a road.*

   SAMPLE 2-POINT RESPONSE:

   • *He picked a different way to go that not many people walked on and it made a difference in his life.*

   SAMPLE 3-POINT RESPONSE:

   • *This poem shows the importance of taking your own path in life and trying something different, not always being a follower.*

2. **Use your own words to describe what you think the author means by . . .**

   SAMPLE 1-POINT RESPONSE:

   • *He took the path less taken and got lost.*

   SAMPLE 2-POINT RESPONSE:

   • *The man went the way most people wouldn't go, and he might have discovered new things.*

   SAMPLE 3-POINT RESPONSE:

   • *I think that the author meant he had different experiences in his life because of the choice he made. The roads represent paths in his life, not actual roads.*

3. **What does the poem tell us about the idea of change? Support with details.**

   SAMPLE 1-POINT RESPONSE:

   • *A road gets weedy when it's not being used.*

   SAMPLE 2-POINT RESPONSE:

   • *He changes his own life by going down a different road. It says "that has made all the difference."*

   SAMPLE 3-POINT RESPONSE:

   • *The choices people make can make big changes in their lives. The person in the poem made a choice that was a big change in his life, and anytime you make a choice between two "roads" you may see lots of changes afterwards.*

4. **Create a title for this poem. Give two reasons from the poem for your new title.**

SAMPLE 1-POINT RESPONSE:

- *A good title would be "The Road in the Wood." This is a good title because the poem's about two roads in the wood.*

SAMPLE 2-POINT RESPONSE:

- *The Road Taken. Because he really talks about how the road he took made a difference for him.*

SAMPLE 3-POINT RESPONSE:

- *Which Path? Because the poem talks about how he stood for a while and had to make a decision, which happens a lot when you have to choose. Also I like the question title because it captures the reader more.*

Pre-Assessment for Writing

(Handout 1B)

NAME: _____ DATE: _____

Directions: Write a paragraph to answer the question below. State your opinion, include three reasons for your opinion, and write a conclusion to your paragraph.

Do you think the poem, "The Road Not Taken," should be required reading for all students in your grade?

Persuasive Writing Scoring Rubric for Pre- and Post-Assessments

Claim or Opinion

Score	Description of Response
0	No clear position exists on the writer's assertion, preference, or view, and context does not help clarify it.
2	Yes/no alone or writer's position is poorly formulated, but reader is reasonably sure what the paper is about because of context.
4	A basic topic sentence exists, and the reader is reasonably sure what the paper is about based on the strength of the topic sentence alone.
6	A very clear, concise position is given as a topic sentence, and the reader is very certain what the paper is about. Must include details such as grade level, title of the reading, or reference to "the story," etc.

Data or Supporting Points

Score	Description of Response
0	No data are offered that are relevant to the claim.
2	Scant data (one or two pieces) are offered, but what data exist are relevant to the claim.
4	At least three pieces of data are offered. They are relevant but not necessarily convincing or complete.
6	At least three pieces of accurate and convincing data are offered.

Warrant or Elaboration on Data

Score	Description of Response
0	No warrant or elaboration is offered.
2	An attempt is made to elaborate at least one element of the data.
4	More than one piece of data is explained, but the explanation is weak and lacks thoroughness, **or** one piece of data is well elaborated.
6	The writer explains more than one piece of data in such a way that it is clear how they support the argument. At least one piece of data is convincingly and completely elaborated.

(Adapted from N. Burkhalter, 1995)

Conclusion

Score	Description of Response
0	No conclusion/closing sentence is provided.
2	A conclusion/closing sentence is provided.

Sample Student Responses
Pre-Assessment for Writing

Sample 1

Yes it should because it's a good rhyming poem by a famous poet. Kids should read poetry by famous poets like Robert Frost because they'll learn more about writing their own poems.

Score: Claim = 2   Total Score = 6
        Data = 2
        Warrant = 2
        Conclusion = 0

Sample 2

Yes, I think the poem should be required reading. It is not too long, and it can teach you a lesson about making choices in your life. It also has some good vocabulary words that can help kids learn. That's why I think it should be required.

Score: Claim = 4   Total Score = 12
        Data = 4
        Warrant = 2
        Conclusion = 2

Sample 3

This poem should not be required reading, in my opinion. It's too short for sixth grade students to read. We usually read longer things in the sixth grade, like stories and novels. Also, the poem doesn't really tell you what happens. You don't know if it was a good road or a bad road, just that it made a difference. Those are my reasons why the poem shouldn't be required.

Score: Claim = 4   Total Score = 12
        Data = 2
        Warrant = 4
        Conclusion = 2

Sample 4

"The Road Not Taken" should be required reading for all students in my grade. It shows you how sometimes you have to make choices in your life and that they will change what happens to you. This is a good lesson for kids to learn. It also has a good lesson that you should not always follow the crowd and do what everybody else does. Some kids just do what all their friends do and don't decide things for themselves, so they ought to listen to what Robert Frost has to say. The poem is also good because it is short so it doesn't take too long to read, and it has good vocabulary like diverge.

Score: Claim = 6   Total Score = 18
         Data = 6
         Warrant = 6
         Conclusion = 0

Independent Reading Assignment for Group A

(Handout 1C)

NAME: _____ DATE: _____

During this unit, you will be reading books from four different cultural groups and discussing the personal and social changes the books demonstrate. As you read each book, think about the questions listed at the bottom of the page, and then respond to them in writing.

Book One—Asian-American

Dragonwings, by Laurence Yep

Book Two—African-American

Roll of Thunder, Hear My Cry, by Mildred Taylor

Book Three—Hispanic-American

Going Home, by Nicholasa Mohr

Book Four—Native American

Morning Star, Black Sun: The Northern Cheyenne Indians and America's Energy Crisis, by Brent Ashabranner

Think about the questions below as you read. Make some notes to yourself about specific parts of the book which relate to each question. After you finish each book, write a paragraph to respond to each of the questions.

▼ *What are the important issues which affect the cultural group represented in this book? In what ways are these issues common to all groups? In what ways are they specific to the group?*

▼ *How is the central issue/problem of the main character or an interviewee developed and resolved?*

▼ *What qualities of the main character or interviewee do you most admire? Why?*

▼ *How does this book help you understand and appreciate cultural differences?*

Independent Reading Assignment
for Group B
(Handout 1D)

NAME: _____ DATE: _____

During this unit, you will be reading books from four different cultural groups and discussing the personal and social changes the books demonstrate. As you read each book, think about the questions listed at the bottom of the page, and then respond to them in writing.

Book One—Asian-American

Journey to Topaz, by Yoshiko Uchida

Book Two—African-American

The Secret of Gumbo Grove, by Eleanora E. Tate

Book Three—Hispanic-American

Taking Sides, by Gary Soto

Book Four—Native American

Rising Voices: Writings of Young Native Americans, by Arlene B. Hirschfelder and Beverly R. Singer

Think about the questions below as you read. Make some notes to yourself about specific parts of the book which relate to each question. After you finish each book, write a paragraph to respond to each of the questions.

▼ *What are the important issues which affect the cultural group represented in this book? In what ways are these issues common to all groups? In what ways are they specific to the group?*

▼ *How is the central issue/problem of the main character or an interviewee developed and resolved?*

▼ *What qualities of the main character or interviewee do you most admire? Why?*

▼ *How does this book help you understand and appreciate cultural differences?*

LESSON

2

▼

The Concept of Change

CURRICULUM ALIGNMENT CODE

GOAL 1	GOAL 2	GOAL 3	GOAL 4	GOAL 5	GOAL 6
	X				X

INSTRUCTIONAL PURPOSE

▼ To introduce the concept of change.

MATERIALS USED

1. Change Model (Handout 2A)

2. Large paper and markers

ACTIVITIES

1. Explain to students that they will be reflecting on the **concept of change** in literature and in their own lives as they explore this unit. Divide students into groups of four or five and distribute large paper and markers to each group. Use the following questions to guide an introductory discussion about change. In their groups, students should discuss the questions and record ideas on the large paper for sharing with the class. Each section of the small group activity should be followed by a brief, whole-class discussion.

Brainstorm ideas about change and write down all responses.

▼ *What ideas come to mind when you think about change?*

▼ *What kinds of things change? What is it about them that changes?*

▼ *How do you know when something has changed? What evidence do you look for to determine whether a change has occurred?*

Categorize the ideas that were written down, putting them into groups and giving each group a title.

▼ *How could you categorize these ideas into groups?*

▼ *What could you call each group? Why?*

▼ *Do all of your changes fall into groups? Might some of them belong in more than one group?*

▼ *Is there a different way you might categorize your ideas? What other categories might you use?*

▼ *What are some of the characteristics of change, based on the ideas you have written?*

Brainstorm a list of things that do not change.

▼ *What are some things that do not change? What are some things that always seem the same or always happen the same way?*

▼ *What evidence or proof do you have that these things do not change?*

▼ *How might you group the things that do not change? What can you call each of these groups?*

▼ *How are the groups of things that do not change similar to or different from the groups of things that do change?*

▼ *Think about the following ideas and whether they show change: routines or habits, rules and regulations, table manners, laws, customs of cultures. Explain your answers. If they show change, where would they fit into your categories of changes? If they do not, where would they fit into your categories of things that do not change?*

Make generalizations about change.

▼ *A **generalization** is something that is always or almost always true. What generalizations can you make about change? Use your examples and categories to guide your thinking, and write several statements that are generalizations about change.*

2. After students share their generalizations about change, introduce the following list and have students compare it to their own set. Explain that the list below is the core set of generalizations that will be used in the unit. Discuss each idea, using the suggested questions as a guide and referring students to their own lists of things that change.

▼ *Change is linked to time. (How is change linked to time? Are all changes linked to time in the same way? How do some of the changes you listed relate to time?)*

▼ *Change may be positive or negative. (What is progress? Does change always represent progress? How might a change be thought of as both positive and negative?)*

▼ *Change may be perceived as orderly or random. (Can we predict change? Select specific changes from your list, and describe which aspects of them can be predicted and which are unpredictable. Even when we know a change will take place, can we always predict exactly how things will turn out?)*

▼ *Change is everywhere. (Does change apply to all areas of our world? What are some specific changes which are universal, or happen everywhere, and some specific changes that may apply to only a smaller area at a given time?)*

▼ *Change may happen naturally or be caused by people. (What causes change? What influence do people have over changes in nature? What influence does nature have over the changes people intend?)*

3. Discuss the following question regarding change: How do our five generalizations about change apply or not apply to the things listed below?

   ▼ *non-living things (e.g., a chair, a pair of scissors)*

   ▼ *traditions (e.g., special holidays, celebrations of birth, passage, and death)*

   ▼ *religious rituals (e.g., celebrations of Christmas or Hanukkah)*

   ▼ *universal truths (e.g., all living things die; all triangles have three sides)*

4. Have students work in their groups to complete the **Change Model** (Handout 2A). (Note: It may be preferable to allow students to copy the model onto larger paper for this activity.) Encourage students to write examples that support each of the five generalizations about change. Provide time for groups to share their ideas with the class. Completed **Change Models** may be displayed in the classroom, and students should also keep copies in their notebooks for reference and additions throughout the unit.

5. Explain that we will be investigating many aspects of change as we explore the unit, including changes in our own lives and society as well as in the literature we read. Encourage students to think about change and watch for changes in the world around them and in the literature they read that support the five generalizations.

NOTES TO TEACHER

1. *The concept development model employed in this lesson is explained in detail in Section IV, Implementation. Stages of the model may be expanded as necessary for adequate development of student understanding.*

2. *This unit is the fourth in a series, and some students may have participated in a concept development activity around change in a previous unit. Nevertheless, teachers are encouraged to work through the model with students again because of the new insights students may bring to a further exploration of the meaning of change.*

3. *Lessons throughout the unit will refer to the list of generalizations included in this lesson. These generalizations should be posted in the classroom, and students should keep their Change Models in their notebooks for reference throughout the unit. The generalizations developed by students should be aligned to this set and may also be posted and used for reference throughout the unit.*

HOMEWORK

1. Write a five-paragraph essay arguing that **one** of the five generalizations about change is true. Give at least three reasons to support your main idea, and explain your reasons carefully. Include a conclusion in your essay.

2. Continue reading the novels you were assigned in Lesson 1.

EXTENSIONS

1. Look through a newspaper or magazine. Find some articles that talk about change. Read one and determine which of the generalizations about change it supports.

2. Interview a person who has lived in more than one country. Ask this person to compare the types of changes they have experienced in the two countries.

PERSUASION

Change Model
(Handout 2A)

NAME: _____ DATE: _____

Develop a list of three–five examples for each of the following statements (generalizations) about change.

Change is linked to time:

Change is everywhere:

Change

Change may be positive:

. . . or negative:

Change may be perceived as orderly:

. . . or random:

Change may happen naturally:

or may be caused by people:

3

Introduction to Grammar and Vocabulary Study

CURRICULUM ALIGNMENT CODE

GOAL 1	GOAL 2	GOAL 3	GOAL 4	GOAL 5	GOAL 6
X		X			

INSTRUCTIONAL PURPOSE

▼ To administer the pre-assessment for grammar.

▼ To introduce the study of grammar.

▼ To develop analytical and interpretive skills in literature.

▼ To explore new vocabulary words.

MATERIALS USED

1. Grammar Pre-Assessment (from Section III, Grammar Study)

2. Word Sort Activity (Handout 3A)

3. Student copies of Grammar Study section (see Section III)

4. "The Road Not Taken" by Robert Frost

5. Literature Web—Teacher Example

6. Literature Web (Handout 3B)

7. Student Response Journals

8. Vocabulary Web—Teacher Example

9. Vocabulary Web (Handout 3C)

10. Dictionaries (Recommended dictionary: *The American Heritage Dictionary of the English Language* (3rd ed.). (1992). Boston: Houghton Mifflin.)

ACTIVITIES

1. Administer **Grammar Pre-Assessment** (found in Grammar Study, Section III) and collect.

2. Give a copy of the **Word Sort Activity** (Handout 3A) to small groups of students. Ask them to cut the words apart. Have them arrange the words in piles according to categories that they think are suitable for the words.

3. Discuss the categories that students have chosen. If they have not sorted by the traditional eight parts of speech, introduce them as a means of sorting. Ask students to re-sort their words according to the eight parts of speech.

4. Review word piles for accuracy in categorization by part of speech.

Key Based on Parts of Speech

(verbs)	(nouns)	(conjunctions)	(adjectives)
a. make	b. table	c. and	d. jolly
sit	book	but	real
open	teacher	or	three
grow	sailboat	nor	best
hear	moon	although	yellow

(adverbs)	(pronouns)	(interjections)	(prepositions)
e. really	f. he	g. aha	h. in
so	she	wow	at
nicely	it	oh	from
too	they	ugh	by
rapidly	we	hello	to

5. Have groups make up sentences using words from as many categories as possible. Share sentences and discuss how the different categories of words function in the sentences. Discuss how some words might be used as more than one part of speech and how one might determine in what sense a word is being used.

6. Distribute to students copies of **Inspecting Our Own Ideas, Student Grammar Study** (from Section III, Grammar Study). Explain that students will be expected to work through parts of this section on their own throughout the course of the unit, with opportunities to ask questions and practice analyzing the structure of sentences in class as well.

7. Return students' attention to "The Road Not Taken" by Robert Frost. Explain that in studying literature, one should carefully explore the meaning of the language used and the literature piece as a whole, and that throughout the unit students will be using several tools to examine literature in these ways. Introduce à **Literature Web** (Handout 3B) as a way of helping students to think about and discuss a piece of literature. Using the **Litera-**

ture Web—Teacher Example and the questions below as a guide, encourage students to fill in and discuss copies of the web for "The Road Not Taken."

   a. **Key Words:** Think and look back over the poem. What were some words or phrases that you especially noticed or thought were really important? Why were they significant to you? Why do you think the poet chose those particular words?

   b. **Feelings:** What feelings did you get when you read the poem? What words contributed to those feelings? What feelings do you think the poet was trying to express? Why? How do you think the speaker felt in the poem? How do you know?

   c. **Ideas:** What was the main idea or theme of the poem? What other ideas was the poet trying to share? What was the poet saying about choices? About change?

   d. **Images and Symbols:** What was the central symbol of the poem? What deeper meaning did the roads have? What other images contributed to the poem and its meaning?

   e. **Structure:** What type of writing is the piece? What poetic structures and devices were used? Examine the punctuation of the poem. How does the separation of the sentences relate to the meaning of the poem? Find words and phrases that are repeated. How does the repetition contribute to the poem?

8. Have students establish a section of their notebook to be used as a **Response Journal** for brief writing assignments throughout the unit. Have students write a response to the following question:

    ▼ *In the poem, Frost mentions that "way leads on to way," suggesting that the choices we make and the roads we take lead us to different choices about different roads. Describe a time in your life when a choice you made led you to another, unexpected path. (Example: Because I decided to play soccer instead of basketball, I met my best friend and won a championship trophy.)*

9. Explain to students that an understanding of vocabulary is very important for an understanding of literature, as well as for one's own writing. Introduce a **Vocabulary Web**. Use the **Teacher Example** following the lesson to guide discussion. Put students in groups of no more than four, with a dictionary available as a resource in each group. Distribute copies of a blank **Vocabulary Web** (Handout 3C) and ask students to write the word *diverge* in the center. Ask students to locate the word in "The Road Not Taken" and write the sentence in which the word appears in the "Sentence" cell of the Vocabulary Web.

10. Have students locate the definition of this word in the dictionary and write it in the "Definition" cell. Have them use the dictionary and/or thesaurus to find synonyms and antonyms for the word to write into the appropriate cells. They should then add the word's part of speech to the appropriate cell.

11. Have students work through the different parts of the "Analysis" section of the web. Encourage them to use the dictionary to help them to think about the *stems* of the word, or the smaller words and pieces of words from which the larger word is made, and fill them into the appropriate cell. (This includes prefixes, suffixes, root words, etc.) Then have students locate the origin of the word (Latin, French, Greek, etc.) in the definition. For the "Word Families" cell, ask students to think of other words which use one or more of the same stems as *diverge*.

12. Ask student groups to develop their own sentences, analogies, or other types of examples using the word for the "Example" cell.

13. Introduce to students the first **Learning Centers** of the unit.

   a. **Language Study Center**

   This Learning Center is intended to provide students with additional opportunities to study language. A set of teacher-made task cards should be kept at the Center with short tasks or projects for students; they may keep a record in their notebooks of task card responses. Task cards may include several activities with different levels of difficulty, and points or scores may be assigned accordingly if the teacher chooses. Several sample task cards are listed below:

   Card 1: *Write the sentence below on a card. Ask at least ten people to read it out loud. Note the way they pronounce the word "February." Look up the pronunciation in a good dictionary. Write a paragraph telling about your "pronunciation survey" and its results.*

   Valentine's Day comes in February.

   Card 2: *Make two word banks that list words that can be used to describe the actions of a) drinking and b) eating. Then substitute an appropriate form of each into the following sentence to see how much difference each makes in the meaning.*

   Alfred _____ the milk and _____ the cookies.

   Card 3: *Look for some words that do not contain the letters **a, e, i, o**, or **u**. List them.*

   Card 4: *Look up the word "anagram" in a dictionary.*

   a) *Write the definition.*

   b) *Analyze the meaning of the word using the Latin meanings of the parts of the word.*

   c) *Make a list of 20 pairs of words that are anagram pairs.*

   Card 5: *Look up the meanings of the words "further" and "farther." Write an explanation of how each should be used. Then write each one in a sentence.*

b. Unit Vocabulary Center

At this Learning Center, a list of new vocabulary words encountered in the unit readings should be kept and regularly updated. (See Introduction to Section II for a list of words.) Dictionaries and blank copies of the Vocabulary Web should be kept at the Center, as well as copies of student readings. Students visiting the Center may work alone or in small groups to develop Vocabulary Webs from unit words, either compiling individual notebooks of webs or a class notebook. This Center allows students to gain more practice with the Vocabulary Web, as class time will not allow all of the new words to be studied in depth.

NOTES TO TEACHER

1. *The grammar pre- and post-assessments may be modified for use with any particular literature selection by changing the words in the sentences to correspond with characters and events in the reading.*

2. *The grammar section of the unit may require more direct teaching than is indicated here, depending on the particular students. Teachers may assign the grammar section as a self-study project for the unit or may choose to add specific lessons on points of grammar. A post-assessment for grammar will be given in Lesson 22, by which time students should have completed the study packet.*

3. *The Literature Web and Vocabulary Web models are also explained in Section IV, Implementation. Teachers should examine vocabulary words to be assigned in order to assist students with the Vocabulary Web. Some cells of the web may not be appropriate for some words.*

4. *Encourage students to keep a vocabulary section in their unit notebooks in which they may write words unfamiliar to them as they read. They should be responsible for locating definitions for these words to help them in their understanding of reading, and they may be asked to complete Vocabulary Webs for some of the words they find.*

HOMEWORK

1. Identify the form (part of speech) of each of the underlined words in the selection from "The Road Not Taken" below:

> And both that morning <u>equally</u> lay
> <u>In</u> leaves no step had trodden black.
> <u>Oh</u>, I kept the first for another day!
> Yet knowing how way leads on to way,
> I doubted if I should ever come back.

<u>I</u> shall be telling this with a sigh
Somewhere ages and ages hence:
<u>Two</u> <u>roads</u> diverged in a wood, and I—
I <u>took</u> the one less traveled by,
<u>And</u> that has made all the difference.

2. Begin the Grammar Study packet.

3. Read the selection from *The Adventures of Tom Sawyer* by Mark Twain.

PERSUASION

Grammar Handout
(Handout 3A)

NAME: _____ DATE: _____

MAKE	TABLE	AND	JOLLY
REALLY	HE	AHA	IN
SIT	BOOK	BUT	REAL
SO	WOW	AT	SHE
OPEN	TEACHER	OR	THREE
NICELY	IT	OH	FROM
GROW	SAILBOAT	NOR	BEST
TOO	THEY	UGH	BY
HEAR	MOON	ALTHOUGH	YELLOW
RAPIDLY	WE	HELLO	TO

Literature Web—Teacher Example

(See Section IV, Implementation, for full explanation)

Key Words
- roads
- diverged
- traveler
- difference

Feelings
- confidence
- sorrow
- doubt
- resignation

Reading
"The Road Not Taken"
by
Robert Frost

Ideas
- decisions
- freedom
- independence
- individuality

Images or Symbols
- two roads
- yellow woods
- traveler
- diverging

Structure
- rhyme pattern same across stanzas
- simple language
- repetition of first line

Literature Web

(Handout 3B)

NAME: _____ DATE: _____

Key Words

Feelings

Reading

Ideas

Images or Symbols

Structure

Vocabulary Web—Teacher Example
(See Section IV, Implementation, for full explanation)

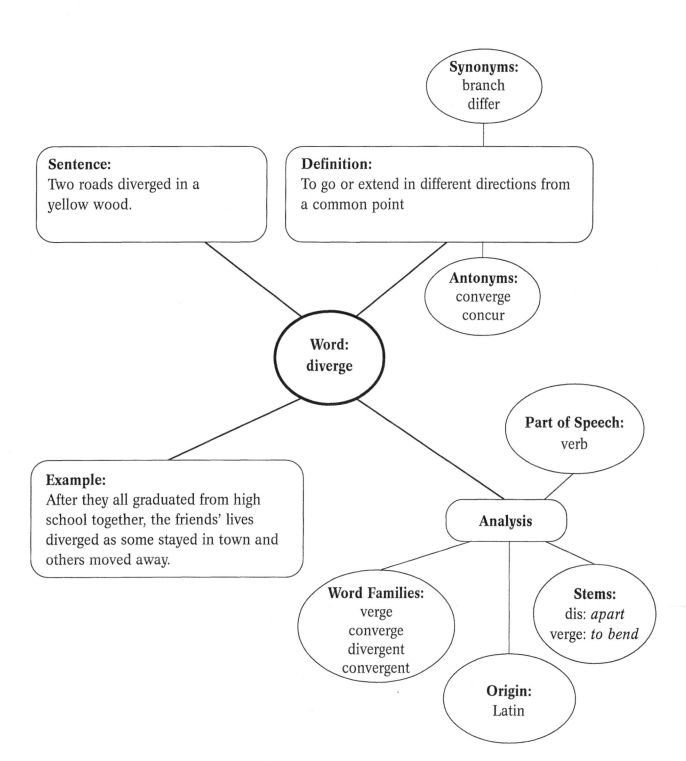

Synonyms:
branch
differ

Sentence:
Two roads diverged in a
yellow wood.

Definition:
To go or extend in different directions from
a common point

Antonyms:
converge
concur

Word:
diverge

Part of Speech:
verb

Example:
After they all graduated from high
school together, the friends' lives
diverged as some stayed in town and
others moved away.

Analysis

Word Families:
verge
converge
divergent
convergent

Stems:
dis: *apart*
verge: *to bend*

Origin:
Latin

PERSUASION

Vocabulary Web
(Handout 3C)

NAME: _____ DATE: _____

Synonyms:

Sentence:

Definition:

Antonyms:

Word:

Part of Speech:

Example:

Analysis

Word Families:

Stems:

Origin:

LESSON

4

▼

The Adventures of Tom Sawyer and the Idea of Persuasion

CURRICULUM ALIGNMENT CODE

GOAL 1	GOAL 2	GOAL 3	GOAL 4	GOAL 5	GOAL 6
X		X	X	X	X

INSTRUCTIONAL PURPOSE

▼ To develop analytical and interpretive skills in literature.

▼ To develop an understanding of persuasion.

MATERIALS USED

1. Selection from *The Adventures of Tom Sawyer* by Mark Twain

2. Literature Web (Handout 4A)

3. Note cards

4. Vocabulary Web (Handout 4B)

5. Student Response Journals

ACTIVITIES

1. Students will have read the selection from *The Adventures of Tom Sawyer* (homework from Lesson 3). Have students independently complete a **Literature Web** (Handout 4A) on the selection, and then share in small groups.

2. Discuss the webs as a class, and then use the following questions to continue discussion about the selection.

Literary Response and Interpretation Questions

▼ *What adjectives would you use to describe the character of Tom Sawyer, based upon this excerpt of the novel? What evidence from the story supports your description?*

▼ *What was Tom's "great, magnificent inspiration"? How did he "put the thing in a new light"?*

▼ *Tom found the world "not so hollow" after all. What does he mean by that statement?*

▼ *How does Aunt Polly perceive Tom? In what ways is this different from how he perceives himself? Are either of their perceptions more accurate? Why or why not?*

▼ *What title might you give to this selection from the book? Give reasons for your selection.*

Reasoning Questions

▼ *What was Tom's problem? What was his first solution? What was his second solution?*

▼ *How were the consequences of Tom's eventual solution different from the consequences he would have faced if Jim had agreed to trade places with him? Which solution was a better one for Tom?*

▼ *Tom's solution to his problem was based on certain assumptions or guesses he made about the other boys. What did Tom assume about the other boys? What is meant by the words, "He had discovered a great law of human action, without knowing it—namely, that in order to make a man or a boy covet a thing, it is only necessary to make the thing difficult to attain"?*

▼ *Would you have been persuaded by Tom's argument? Why or why not?*

Change Questions

▼ *What techniques did Tom use to change people's minds?*

▼ *Would you classify the changes that took place in the story as positive or negative for the people involved? Why? In what ways was the white-washing arrangement thought to be positive by everyone?*

▼ *How does the classification of something as work or as play change the way you feel about it?*

3. Discuss *persuasion* as an important aspect of this unit. Write the word *persuasion* on the board and have students brainstorm ideas about what persuasion is. Write the list on the board and discuss. Have a student read the definition of *persuasion* from the dictionary, and compare the definition to the list generated by the class.

4. Ask students to brainstorm a list of chores they are responsible for at home. Each student should then choose one chore and prepare a one-minute speech to persuade another member of the class to want to do the task, as Tom persuaded his friends to want to do his chore. Give the following directions as guidelines for preparing for the speech:

   A. Clearly describe what the chore is, in a way that makes it seem attractive to someone who might have to do it.

   B. Give at least three reasons to persuade someone else to do the chore.

   C. Make an outline of your description and persuasive reasons on note cards.

5. Have students present their persuasive speeches, speaking from their note cards. After the speeches, have students vote as to whether they would have been persuaded to do the chores or not and why.

6. Have students work in small groups to complete a **Vocabulary Web** (Handout 4B) for one of the following words from the *Tom Sawyer* chapter: **delectable, melancholy, expeditions, straitened, laborious, ponderously, circumstance, philosopher**. Discuss the completed webs.

7. Give students the following sentence from the chapter. Ask them to identify the part of speech of each underlined word and its function in the sentence. Provide time for students to ask questions about their independent grammar study.

   Saturday morning <u>was come</u>, <u>and</u> all the summer <u>world</u> was bright and <u>fresh</u>, and <u>brimming</u> with life.

8. Have students respond to one of the following questions in their **Response Journals**:

   ▼ *Have you ever outwitted someone? Describe the occasion and how you managed to fool another person.*

   ▼ *What are some tasks you enjoy doing that others might think of as work? What are some things you think of as work which might seem like play to someone else?*

HOMEWORK

Continue working on your independent reading and writing assignment from Lesson 1. The discussion of the Asian-American books will take place in Lesson 7.

EXTENSIONS

1. Read *The Adventures of Tom Sawyer* by Mark Twain. Make a chart showing how the characters change over the course of the novel.

2. Play the game *Persuade.** In this game, each group of six students receives a set of "audience," "audience background," and "persuasion goal" cards. To begin, a set of cards is drawn and the audience role plays according to the "audience" and "audience background" directions. The persuader then delivers a four-minute speech to persuade his or her audience. Following the speech, the audience has three minutes to ask questions. At the conclusion of each round, participants rate the speaker using score sheets.

*Kienzle, N. K. (1981). *Persuade.* [Game]. Colorado Springs, CO: Meriwether/Contemporary Drama.

PERSUASION

Literature Web
(Handout 4A)

NAME: _____ DATE: _____

Key Words

Feelings

Reading

Ideas

Images or
Symbols

Structure

Vocabulary Web
(Handout 4B)

NAME: _____ DATE: _____

Synonyms:

Sentence:

Definition:

Antonyms:

Word:

Part of Speech:

Example:

Analysis

Word Families:

Stems:

Origin:

65

5

The Hamburger Model of Persuasive Writing

CURRICULUM ALIGNMENT CODE

GOAL 1	GOAL 2	GOAL 3	GOAL 4	GOAL 5	GOAL 6
	X			X	

INSTRUCTIONAL PURPOSE

▼ To introduce persuasive writing through use of the Hamburger Model.

MATERIALS USED

1. Why You Should Become a Vegetarian (Handout 5A)

2. Hamburger Model of Persuasive Writing (Handout 5B)

3. Jumbled Paragraph (Handout 5C)

ACTIVITIES

1. Explain that persuasion can be done in a variety of ways. One of those ways is by writing. Share the example paragraph about **Why You Should Become a Vegetarian** (Handout 5A) with students. You may give out individual copies or make a transparency and have students read it together as you display it on an overhead projector.

2. Share the **Hamburger Model of Persuasive Writing** (Handout 5B). Explain that it is not the only model for writing a paragraph but that it works well for giving an opinion in written form. Ask students to compare the sample paragraph discussed above with the structure used in the model, and to identify specific pieces of the paragraph which represent elements of the Hamburger Model. Use the following questions as a guide for the discussion:

▼ *What is the "top bun" or topic and opinion statement of the paragraph?*

▼ *What is the writer's "meat" or supporting information? How many reasons does the author provide? Are they convincing reasons?*

> ▼ *How did the writer add details and examples or extra "fixings" to the paragraph?*
>
> ▼ *What is the "bottom bun" or conclusion to the paragraph?*

3. Give out the **Jumbled Paragraph** (Handout 5C) and ask students to work in small groups to rearrange the pieces, using the Hamburger Model as a guide. Have one group share their completed paragraph with the whole class, and invite others to share whether they agree or disagree with the arrangement and why. Discuss the reasoning that helped unscramble the paragraph, including consideration of "clue words." Relate this paragraph back to the Hamburger Model, asking which sentences represent which pieces of the model and whether all necessary pieces are included. Ask students to suggest ways they might improve the paragraph to make it more convincing or interesting.

4. Have students work in small groups to write Hamburger Model paragraphs arguing a point of view about whether students should receive rewards for good grades in school. When groups have completed their paragraphs, they may copy their work onto overhead transparencies for sharing with the class.

5. Ask groups of students to share their paragraphs, and invite listeners to identify elements of the structure and to discuss how convincing the paragraphs are.

6. Introduce a unit **Writing Computer Center**. At this Learning Center, students have the opportunity to practice the stages of writing and the format of the persuasive paragraph. Writing materials and a word processing program should be made available to students along with a list of suggested writing topics. Students may compose paragraphs and longer pieces at the Writing Computer Center, may work in pairs to critique one another's work, and may revise, edit, and publish their work. This Center may be used to work on unit assignments and/or on separate extension activities.

NOTES TO TEACHER

1. *The Hamburger Model is also explained in Section IV, Implementation. It may be helpful to keep an enlarged copy of the Model posted in the classroom for reference throughout the unit.*

2. *Here is the key to the Jumbled Paragraph:*

   I think that the use of calculators in middle school classrooms is a good thing. First, the use of the calculator allows students to do more challenging problems that emphasize thinking rather than computation. By middle school, students should have already learned the basics of computation and even if they didn't, they should move on to more important problem-solving skills. Also, the calculator allows you to solve problems that don't have easy numbers. Big numbers, decimals, square roots, and long columns of numbers can be handled more easily. Thirdly, using a calculator is a skill that is important in adult life and needs to be practiced. Adults use calculators in their jobs and for household tasks such as balancing their checkbooks. As you can see, there are many good reasons for using calculators in middle school math classes.

HOMEWORK

Imagine the following to be true in your school: The student government has been given $500 for the purpose of doing something to benefit the school. Take a point of view on how you think the money should be spent and write a paragraph defending your opinion, using the Hamburger Model.

PERSUASION

Why You Should Become a Vegetarian

(Handout 5A)

NAME: _____ DATE: _____

    I believe that more people should become vegetarians for many reasons. Most importantly, eating meat hurts defenseless animals. They are often raised and transported in uncomfortable conditions and then they are killed. There are also health reasons not to eat meat. Studies show that vegetarians are less likely to have heart disease and cancer. A third reason is that it takes more natural resources to raise meat than other foods such as fruits and vegetables. Not only do you have to raise the cattle, you have to raise the food to feed the cattle. For these reasons I hope that people who eat meat will rethink their eating habits and consider becoming vegetarian.

PERSUASION

Hamburger Model for Persuasive Writing

(Handout 5B)

NAME: _____ DATE: _____

Introduction
(State your opinion.)

Elaboration

Elaboration

Elaboration

Reasons

Reasons

Reasons

Elaboration

Elaboration

Elaboration

Conclusion

Jumbled Paragraph

(Handout 5C)

NAME: _____ DATE: _____

Calculators: More Power to You!

Also, the calculator allows you to solve problems that don't have easy numbers.

I think that the use of calculators in middle school classrooms is a good thing.

As you can see, there are many good reasons for using calculators in middle school math classes.

By middle school, students should have already learned the basics of computation and even if they didn't, they should move on to more important problem-solving skills and let the calculator do the number crunching for them.

Thirdly, using a calculator is a skill that is important in adult life and needs to be practiced.

Big numbers, decimals, square roots, and long columns of numbers can be handled more easily.

Adults use calculators in their jobs and for household tasks such as balancing their checkbooks.

First, the use of the calculator allows students to do more challenging problems that emphasize thinking rather than computation.

6

Introduction to Persuasive Speaking

CURRICULUM ALIGNMENT CODE

GOAL 1	GOAL 2	GOAL 3	GOAL 4	GOAL 5	GOAL 6
	X		X	X	

INSTRUCTIONAL PURPOSE

▼ To introduce persuasive speaking.

▼ To examine persuasive techniques used in advertising.

MATERIALS USED

1. Oral Presentation Evaluation Form (Handout 6A)

2. Note cards

3. Magazine advertisements

4. Student Response Journals

ACTIVITIES

1. Remind students of the effectiveness of Tom's oral persuasion in the selection from *The Adventures of Tom Sawyer.* Explain that throughout the unit, students will be asked to give persuasive speeches on various topics. As an introduction to oral persuasion, students will give a short oral presentation persuading classmates to read a book. Introduce the **Oral Presentation Evaluation Form** (Handout 6A), and discuss important things to remember when giving speeches, such as using notes to keep track of your points and making eye contact with the audience.

2. Give each student a note card and the following directions:

    A. Think of one of your favorite books and why you like it.

    B. On your note card, write the title, author, and reasons that other students should read the book.

C. Share your information with the class in a one-minute speech. Think about the suggestions on the **Oral Presentation Evaluation Form** as you prepare and present your speech.

3. Put these cards in alphabetical order by titles in a file box for the beginning of a file of "class favorite books" to be added to throughout the unit. It may then serve as a source for others to use in choosing independent reading material. Have students who select the book later use the back of the synopsis card to record why they chose to read it. Have them indicate whether their decision was based on the card, the speech, the synopsis of the book on its cover, or something else. Have them state which words and/or pictures persuaded them to choose to read that particular book.

4. Have students work in groups of 3–4 to discuss persuasive advertisement techniques. Give each group a selection of different types of advertisements from print sources. (Examples: advertisements from magazines and newspapers for clothes, foods, drinks, movies, books.) Allow ten minutes for the groups to discuss and list what persuasive techniques have been used in the ads. Have each group share with the class the persuasive techniques they listed. (Examples: color to attract us, use of words, logos, celebrity endorsement, acceptance by others.)

5. Ask students to collect advertisements for Lesson 19. They should bring examples from as many of the following sources as possible: television, radio, junk mail, magazines and newspapers, telephone solicitations, World Wide Web, and billboards. Explain that they will be categorizing ads by the techniques of persuasion used.

6. Have students write in their **Response Journals** in response to these questions:

   ▼ *What changes took place in the Tom Sawyer story? How do these changes support or refute the generalizations about change? How do they relate to the idea of persuasion?*

7. Set up a **Persuasive Speaking Center**. At this Learning Center, have available videos of speeches which students may watch and analyze according to their growing understanding of elements of persuasion. Encourage them to evaluate the speeches they watch, using the materials they are given to evaluate presentations in class. The Center should also have available a list of prompts for persuasive speeches students may develop and deliver themselves to a small group of peers or to the class.

HOMEWORK

1. Finish the Asian-American selection from the independent reading assignment from Lesson 1 and the corresponding response writing in preparation for the next lesson.

2. Begin collecting advertisements for an activity in Lesson 19.

EXTENSION

Read the last paragraph of the selection from *Tom Sawyer*. Think about how you would have felt had you been Tom when Aunt Polly gave you the treat "along with an improving lecture upon the added value and flavor a treat took to itself when it came without sin through virtuous effort." Write about this incident in your **Response Journal**.

Include answers to the following questions:

▼ Would Aunt Polly's lecture change you? Why or why not?

▼ How do you think the lecture affected Tom?

▼ What changes took place in this story?

PERSUASION

Oral Presentation Evaluation Form
(Handout 6A)

SPEAKER: _____ DATE: _____

ASSIGNMENT: _____

Directions: Circle the choice that best describes each of the following.

ORGANIZATION

1. The purpose of the presentation was clear.	Needs Improvement	Satisfactory	Excellent
2. The speaker included effective examples.	Needs Improvement	Satisfactory	Excellent
3. The speaker showed knowledge of the subject.	Needs Improvement	Satisfactory	Excellent
4. The presentation closed with a strong, interesting idea that restated the purpose.	Needs Improvement	Satisfactory	Excellent

DELIVERY

1. The speaker made frequent eye contact with the audience.	Needs Improvement	Satisfactory	Excellent
2. The presentation was loud enough.	Needs Improvement	Satisfactory	Excellent
3. The speaker's words were clear enough to be understood.	Needs Improvement	Satisfactory	Excellent

THE BEST PART OF THIS PRESENTATION WAS:

_____

_____

A SUGGESTION FOR IMPROVEMENT IS:

_____

_____

LESSON

7

Discussion of Asian-American Literature

CURRICULUM ALIGNMENT CODE

GOAL 1	GOAL 2	GOAL 3	GOAL 4	GOAL 5	GOAL 6
X				X	X

INSTRUCTIONAL PURPOSE

▼ To develop analytical and interpretive skills in literature.

MATERIALS USED

1. *Dragonwings* by Laurence Yep

2. *Journey to Topaz* by Yoshiko Uchida

3. Literature Web (Handout 7A)

4. Independent Reading Assignment (Handouts 1C and 1D, from Lesson 1) and students' written responses

5. Cultures and Change Matrix (Handouts 7B and 7C)

ACTIVITIES

1. Divide students according to Group A and Group B (based upon **Independent Reading Assignments** from Lesson 1). Within each group, have students form smaller groups of 4–5 people.

2. Ask each student to complete a **Literature Web** (Handout 7A) independently, based on their reading of an Asian-American literature selection (*Dragonwings* or *Journey to Topaz*).

3. Students should then discuss their webs with their small groups and develop a group web to share with the class. These group webs should be completed on large chart paper or overheads, if possible, so that the class may see and discuss them. Have one member of each group share the group web with the class. .

4. Display the different webs in the classroom, and discuss as a class the similarities and differences among the Group A webs and the Group B webs. Ask students to comment on any common themes they recognize between the two books.

5. Continue discussion of the books, using the following questions as a guide.

Reasoning Questions

▼ *Not only do different cultures have special customs and traditions, they also may perceive the world differently. How does this statement apply to the book you just read?*

▼ *Literature from all cultures employs strong characters to tell a story. What characters from your reading impressed you? Why? Give specific evidence from the book to support your opinion.*

▼ *What inferences can you make about what the characters learned in the book? On what evidence do you base your conclusions?*

▼ *What predictions might you make about the life of your favorite character after the story ends? What data from the books can you provide to support your predictions?*

▼ *Why does the author use a particular cultural group as the context for the story? What purposes does he or she have in doing so?*

▼ *How do the issues in the book relate to problems of society today? What are the implications of these problems for us/you?*

Change Question

▼ *What elements of change are evident in the book you read? How do they support our generalizations on change?*

6. Have students return to their small groups to discuss their written responses to the questions on the **Independent Reading Assignment** (Handouts 1C and 1D, from Lesson 1). Distribute the **Cultures and Change Matrix** (Handouts 7B and 7C) and have students complete the section of the chart which applies to the Asian-American readings. Students should keep this chart in their notebooks to be added to throughout the unit. Teachers may also wish to post a large copy of the chart in the classroom.

HOMEWORK

Read Book Two from the **Independent Reading Assignment** (Handouts 1C and 1D) in preparation for a discussion in Lesson 10.

EXTENSIONS

1. Read the literature selection which was assigned to the other group for this lesson. Compare the two books.

2. Find more books by the author of the book you read. Read several of these books and prepare book reviews about them, with a brief synopsis of the life of the author.

PERSUASION

Literature Web
(Handout 7A)

NAME: _____ DATE: _____

Key Words

Feelings

Reading

Ideas

*Images or
Symbols*

Structure

Cultures and Change Matrix

(Handout 7B)

NAME: _____ DATE: _____

GROUP A

Titles/ Culture	Pervasive	Linked to Time	Systemic or Random	Growth or Regression	Natural Order or Imposed
Dragonwings Asian- American					
Roll of Thunder, Hear My Cry African- American					
Going Home Hispanic- American					
Morning Star, Black Sun . . . Native American					

Cultures and Change Matrix
(Handout 7C)

NAME: _____ DATE: _____

GROUP B

Titles/ Culture	Pervasive	Linked to Time	Systemic or Random	Growth or Regression	Natural Order or Imposed
Journey to Topaz Asian-American					
The Secret of Gumbo Grove African-American					
Taking Sides Hispanic-American					
Rising Voices . . . Native American					

LESSON

8

▼

Reasoning

CURRICULUM ALIGNMENT CODE

GOAL 1	GOAL 2	GOAL 3	GOAL 4	GOAL 5	GOAL 6
	X			X	

INSTRUCTIONAL PURPOSE

▼ To introduce elements of reasoning as part of persuasive writing.

▼ To discuss standards of reasoning for evaluating arguments.

MATERIALS USED

1. Elements of Reasoning (Handout 8A)

2. Why You Should Become a Vegetarian (Handout 5A)

3. Hamburger Paragraph Structure (Handout 8B)

4. Standards of Reasoning (Handout 8C)

ACTIVITIES

1. Review the Hamburger Model for Persuasive Writing with students. Explain that the hamburger structure alone does not guarantee a strong persuasive paragraph. One needs to look carefully at the information and reasons that make up the ideas of the paragraph. Show the **Elements of Reasoning** (Handout 8A) on the overhead projector. Explain that these elements can help us think and argue better, and that we will begin to pay careful attention to some of them in our writing.

2. Examine an example of how the elements of reasoning can be used to analyze the following situation: *You plant 10 azalea bushes in your front yard. Three days later, most of the leaves have disappeared.*

   Use the following questions to discuss what is meant by each element.

   A. **Purpose or Goal:** What was the purpose of planting the bushes? (Examples: for decoration; for erosion control)

93

B. **Issue or Problem:** What is the problem that you are dealing with? (Example: What is causing the leaves to disappear from the bushes, and how can you prevent it from happening in the future?)

C. **Experiences, Data, or Evidence:** What are the facts that will help you make your decision? (Examples: Neighbors say that deer have been eating their plants. You call the county horticultural extension office and they say that deer love azaleas.)

D. **Inferences (or small conclusions):** What are the small conclusions that you make in the decision-making process based on the facts that you have? (Examples: Since there is no evidence of the leaves falling to the ground, something ate the leaves. Since there are deer in the neighborhood, it may be the deer that caused the problem. If the leaves are gone from the bushes, the bushes will not survive.)

E. **Point of View:** What would each of the people involved think about the problem? What is the point of view of the deer? (Example: You want something done to thin the deer herds but you have a neighbor who loves deer and actually puts out cracked corn to attract them.)

F. **Concepts or Ideas:** What ideas are involved in this problem? (Examples: man vs. wildlife; survival)

G. **Assumptions:** What assumptions might you make? (Example: When you planted the azaleas, you assumed that the leaves would stay on and that the bushes would grow.)

H. **Implications and Consequences:** What are the implications for your garden because of the deer? (Example: You can't plant azaleas unless you build a fence or use deer repellents.)

3. Use the questions below and the paragraph called "Why You Should Become a Vegetarian" (Handout 5A) to help students see the relationship of persuasive writing to these elements of reasoning.

▼ *What was the author's purpose in writing this paragraph? What are other purposes for writing?*

▼ *What is the issue that is addressed in this paragraph?*

▼ *What is the point of view of the writer on this issue? What other points of view might someone take on the issue?*

▼ *What evidence is given in the paragraph to support the idea that raising meat consumes more natural resources than raising vegetables? What inference can you make from this about the place of cattle in the food chain?*

▼ *What concept or big idea is addressed in this paragraph? Do you think the concept of animal rights is present in all cultures of the world? Why or why not?*

▼ *What are the consequences for the beef industry if many people adopt a vegetarian diet? What are the implications for restaurants?*

▼ *What assumption does the writer make about the living conditions of animals that are raised for the meat industry?*

4. Revisit the Hamburger Model and overlay "point of view" and "issue" on the top bun, "evidence" and "inferences" in the middle, and "consequences" in the bottom bun (See **Hamburger Paragraph Structure**, Handout 8B). Tell students that these elements are commonly found in the Hamburger Model for Persuasive Writing. Ask them if they are present in the "Why You Should Become a Vegetarian" handout.

5. Introduce the **Standards of Reasoning** (Handout 8C) and discuss the questions students might ask in considering the strength of an argument. Have students use the "Why You Should Become a Vegetarian" handout to discuss the standards. Ask them to consider which of the standards are met and to what degree.

6. Have small groups generate reasons for a paragraph on whether there should be fines imposed for overdue books in the school library. Have them share their ideas in their groups and then ask for volunteers to contribute parts in order to write a class paragraph on the overhead projector. Examine the paragraph structure using the Hamburger Model and the strength of the reasons by using the questions in the Standards of Reasoning handout.

7. Have students review the paragraphs written for homework in Lesson 5 on how money given to the student government should be spent. Ask them to share their paragraphs in groups and consider whether their paragraphs reflect both the Hamburger Model and the Elements of Reasoning. Have them evaluate the paragraphs using the **Standards of Reasoning**. Ask them to revise their paragraphs as prompted by the discussion.

NOTES TO TEACHER

1. *The Elements of Reasoning are outlined in more detail in Section IV, Implementation.*

2. *Students should keep their copies of the **Standards of Reasoning** in their notebooks. They will be referring to the standards numerous times throughout the course of the unit.*

HOMEWORK

Write a hamburger paragraph on the following issue by writing a letter to the editor of your school paper:

Should the Pledge of Allegiance be recited in school? Why or why not?

Evaluate your own paper, using the **Standards of Reasoning**.

EXTENSION

Find an editorial in the newspaper. Critique it using the questions for Standards of Reasoning on Handout 8C.

Elements of Reasoning

(Handout 8A)

NAME: _____ DATE: _____

1. **Purpose or Goal**

2. **Issue or Problem**

3. **Point of View**

4. **Experiences, Data, or Evidence**

5. **Concepts or Ideas**

6. **Assumptions**

7. **Inferences**

8. **Implications and Consequences**

PERSUASION

Hamburger Paragraph Structure
(Handout 8B)

NAME: _____ DATE: _____

Issue
Point of View

Elaboration

Inferences

Elaboration

Reasons

Reasons

Reasons

Inferences

Elaboration

Inferences

Consequences

Standards of Reasoning

(Handout 8C)

NAME: _____ DATE: _____

▼ Are there **enough reasons** to make a convincing argument? One or two reasons might not be enough to show your point of view well enough to be fully understood.

▼ Is the evidence **correct or right**?

▼ Are the reasons **clear**? Is the meaning understandable by anyone who reads this? Are they explained well, or is more information needed?

▼ Are **specific** reasons or examples included rather than vague generalizations?

▼ Are the arguments and reasons **strong and important**? or do they seem to be included just to have something to say?

▼ Is the thinking **logical**? Does the paragraph follow an understandable path or is it just a disconnected group of statements? Do the sentences seem to go together and to be in the right order?

LESSON
9
▼

The Declaration of Independence

CURRICULUM ALIGNMENT CODE

GOAL 1	GOAL 2	GOAL 3	GOAL 4	GOAL 5	GOAL 6
X	X	X		X	X

INSTRUCTIONAL PURPOSE

▼ To develop analytical and interpretive skills in reading historical documents.

▼ To apply the elements of reasoning to an argument.

▼ To explore new vocabulary words.

▼ To develop persuasive writing skills.

MATERIALS USED

1. The Declaration of Independence

2. Elements of Reasoning (Handout 8A)

3. Standards of Reasoning (Handout 8C)

4. Literature Web (Handout 9A)

5. Vocabulary Web (Handout 9B)

6. The Language of Persuasion (Handout 9C)

7. Student Response Journals

ACTIVITIES

1. Lead a discussion with students to determine their background knowledge about the Revolutionary War era and the events surrounding the Second Continental Congress and the Declaration of Independence. Ask students to explain their understanding of the *issues* that faced the Second Continental Congress and the *purpose* for the writing of the Declaration. Have students refer to their copies of the **Elements of Reasoning** (Handout 8A, from Lesson 8) throughout the following activities.

2. Have students read the Declaration and work in pairs to complete a **Literature Web** (Handout 9A) for the document. Discuss the webs as a class, and then use the following questions based on the **Elements of Reasoning** and the **Standards of Reasoning** (Handouts 8A and 8C) to discuss the document further:

▼ *How does Jefferson introduce the purpose of the Declaration within the first few sentences? What words express the point of view of the Continental Congress?*

▼ *Which specific sentences in the introductory part of the document speak of the problem or issue?*

▼ *Why does Jefferson point out that "Prudence, indeed, will dictate that Governments long established should not be changed for light and transient causes"? How does this strengthen his argument?*

▼ *What are some of the specific pieces of evidence Jefferson provides in support of his argument? Use the **Standards of Reasoning** to evaluate the reasons.*

▼ *Does the evidence provided justify Jefferson's claim that King George III was a tyrant, unfit to be the ruler of a free people? Why or why not?*

▼ *Who was the intended audience for the Declaration of Independence? How do you know? How might different audiences have reacted to it?*

▼ *What consequences and implications might this document have had for its authors?*

▼ *How was Thomas Jefferson a change agent in colonial America? How was this document an important catalyst for change?*

3. Have students work in groups to complete a **Vocabulary Web** (Handout 9B) for one or more of the following words from the Declaration of Independence: *unanimous, unalienable, acquiesce, annihilation, perfidy, rectitude, magnanimity, usurpations, consanguinity, despotism, jurisdiction*.

4. Ask students to consider why the Declaration of Independence may be seen as an example of a persuasive writing piece. Have them identify the sections of the document which could represent the parts of the Hamburger Model. Discuss whether the argument presented in the document is effective and why.

5. Explain to students that strong reasons are not always enough to make an argument convincing; the reasons have to be expressed effectively as well. Introduce **The Language of Persuasion** (Handout 9C) and discuss the techniques with regard to the Declaration of Independence, using the questions below as a guide.

A. **Word choice**

▼ *Jefferson uses the words "dissolve the political bands" to describe the efforts toward separation from Great Britain. What efforts were actually taking place to dissolve those bands? Why are the words "rebellion" and "revolution" not used?*

▼ *Find several adjectives used to describe the people of the colonies and adjectives used to describe the British. How do the word choices influence the reader's understanding of events?*

B. **Figurative language**

▼ *Find examples of figurative language in the Declaration. Why does Jefferson use the phrase "swarms of Officers" and compare the actions of the "foreign Mercenaries" to those of "the most barbarous ages"?*

C. **Sentence patterns**

▼ *Look at the series of sentences in which Jefferson outlines the actions of the King. How does each sentence begin? What is the effect of the repetition?*

▼ *Some of the most well-known words of this document are near the beginning— "Life, Liberty, and the pursuit of Happiness"—and at the very end—"our Lives, our Fortunes, and our sacred Honor." What do you notice about the structure of these two phrases? Why do you think they are memorable? Why did Jefferson not include four or five items, or only one or two, in each case? Try to find other examples in the document of phrases which reflect numerical patterns.*

D. **Imitative language patterns**

▼ *Why does Jefferson continually refer to Laws throughout the document?*

E. **Concrete and abstract images**

▼ *Find the instances of the words "tyrant" and "tyranny" in the document. What are the implications of the words? Does Jefferson ever call the King a tyrant directly? Why or why not?*

▼ *Why does Jefferson not refer to any specific dates, events, or colonies in the document? How does he make the words generalizable across the thirteen colonies?*

6. Provide students with additional historical resources about the writing and signing of the Declaration of Independence. In small groups, have students search for answers to the following questions:

▼ *The members of the Continental Congress argued over many of the specific words of the Declaration before signing it. Find out what some of the issues were that they discussed, and consider whether the document is more persuasive as it stands or as it would have stood if the arguments had turned out differently.*

▼ *Find out about the reaction of the people of Philadelphia to the reading of the Declaration on July 8, 1776. Were they persuaded by its words? Find out about the reactions of the other colonies. What was the reaction of the King?*

▼ *What were the consequences for the individual signers of the Declaration of Independence? Find out what became of some of the less well-known of the signers.*

7. Have students respond to the following question in their **Response Journals**:

▼ *Imagine that you were one of the representatives at the Second Continental Congress. Would you have signed the Declaration right away, or would you have still argued about certain pieces of it? Why? What would have persuaded you one way or the other? Write a paragraph to explain your decision and your reasons.*

8. Remind students again of the *purpose* of the Declaration of Independence, and that it was written to be delivered to the King of England and published for the people of the colonies. Have students generate a list of ways that people can share their persuasive messages with others, including through letters to the editor, editorials, advertisements, or letters directly to companies, individuals, etc. Ask students to think about some concerns that they have or issues about which they would like to persuade someone of their opinion. For example, there may be a school or local issue about which students have strong opinions they would like to share. Have each student brainstorm a list of issues that are of concern to them, and beside each issue students should list the name of someone to whom they should write a persuasive letter expressing their opinion on the issue. Tell students that they are to write a rough draft of a persuasive letter in time for Lesson 12. Remind them to use the Hamburger Model and the Standards of Reasoning to guide them as they write their letter.

NOTES TO TEACHER

1. *The Hamburger Model and the Elements of Reasoning should be used to help students structure their reading of the document. An emphasis on structural elements should be somewhat helpful to students in handling the length and unfamiliar language of the Declaration.*

2. *Additional historical resources will be needed to assist students in gaining background knowledge about the Declaration and in completing some of the activities. Numerous books and videotapes are available about the colonial and revolutionary eras, as well as Internet sites which contain useful information. Key search terms to use when looking for such sites include **Philadelphia, Declaration of Independence, American Revolution, and Jefferson.***

3. *The handout on **The Language of Persuasion** (Handout 9C) should be kept in student notebooks for reference throughout the unit. You may also wish to post a copy in the classroom.*

4. *You may choose to have students complete the persuasive letter writing assignment about individual issues of their own choice or about a school or local issue of concern to the class. The issues chosen should be real issues about which students would have genuine concern and about which their letters have some possibility of having an influence. As the overall subject of the unit is persuasion, the object of this assignment is to have students see the effects of persuasion in the real world, not just to complete an exercise. Thus, for example, students may write to the principal about changing the dress code, to the school board about acquiring more computers for classrooms, or to the editor of the local paper about establishing curbside recycling efforts.*

HOMEWORK

1. Finish the African-American selection from the independent reading assignment from Lesson 1 and the corresponding response writing in preparation for the next lesson.

2. Write a rough draft of a persuasive letter for Lesson 12.

EXTENSIONS

1. Do some research on Thomas Jefferson. Read a biography of Jefferson and find out what led him to be part of the Second Continental Congress and how he was chosen to write the Declaration. What other important documents did Jefferson write?

2. Many other groups that have worked for liberty since the time of the American Revolution have used Jefferson's words to inspire their own actions. Find out about other revolutions that have based their own work toward freedom on the Declaration of Independence.

3. Read another famous document of American history, Lincoln's Gettysburg Address. Compare the Gettysburg Address to the Declaration of Independence. How did Lincoln imitate parts of the Declaration in order to make his own speech more effective? (See **The Language of Persuasion**, Handout 9C, item D.) Complete a **Literature Web** for the Gettysburg Address, paying particular attention to key words and to structure.

Literature Web
(Handout 9A)

NAME: _____ DATE: _____

Key Words

Feelings

Reading

Ideas

Images or
Symbols

Structure

Vocabulary Web
(Handout 9B)

NAME: _____ DATE: _____

Synonyms:

Sentence:

Definition:

Antonyms:

Word:

Part of Speech:

Example:

Analysis

Word Families:

Origin:

Stems:

The Language of Persuasion
(Handout 9C)

NAME: _____ DATE: _____

Language is the basis of argument and persuasion. It shapes our thoughts and influences our beliefs and actions. Some of the ways language can be used to persuade and manipulate are listed below.

A. Word choice

▼ Words have both literal and emotional meanings. The emotional meaning of a word is its "connotation." For instance, while *clever* and *cunning* both describe a person as skillful and talented, most people would prefer to be called *clever*, because *cunning* also implies a crafty slyness. Words used in this way are sometimes said to be "loaded," because they are loaded with extra meaning.

▼ Euphemisms, words that make things seem better than they are, use connotations. *Youthful offender* is a euphemism. Other examples include *air support* instead of *bombing* and *intelligence gathering* instead of *spying*.

B. Figurative language

▼ Metaphors, similes, and analogies compare one thing to another, often in startling or unusual ways, to gain the attention or sympathy of the audience. *That salesman sounds like a TV evangelist; you have to have a lot of faith to believe anything he says!*

C. Sentence patterns

▼ Certain sentence patterns—for example, repetition of a key word or phrase—can fire the emotions in either a positive or a negative way.

D. Imitative language patterns

▼ A writer or speaker may use language patterns familiar from other respected sources, such as the Bible or the works of Shakespeare, to evoke similar emotional responses.

E. Concrete and abstract images

▼ Stereotypes are sometimes used to influence listeners. *Nerd* is an example. Generalizations may also be used to persuade. *He was a poor struggling artist.*

Compiled from:

Hirschberg, S. (1990). *Strategies of argument*. New York: Macmillan. pp. 191–212.

Stanford, J. A. (1993). *Connections: A multicultural reader for writers*. Mountain View, CA: Mayfield. p. 408.

LESSON
10
▼

Discussion of African-American Literature

CURRICULUM ALIGNMENT CODE

GOAL 1	GOAL 2	GOAL 3	GOAL 4	GOAL 5	GOAL 6
X				X	X

INSTRUCTIONAL PURPOSE

▼ To develop analytical and interpretive skills in literature.

MATERIALS USED

1. *Roll of Thunder, Hear My Cry* by Mildred Taylor

2. *The Secret of Gumbo Grove* by Eleanora Tate

3. Literature Web (Handout 10A)

4. Independent Reading Assignment (Handouts 1C and 1D, from Lesson 1) and students' written responses

5. Cultures and Change Matrix (Handouts 7B and 7C)

ACTIVITIES

1. Divide students according to Group A and Group B (based upon **Independent Reading Assignments** from Lesson 1). Within each group, have students form smaller groups of 4–5 people.

2. Ask each student to complete a **Literature Web** (Handout 10A) independently, based on their reading of an African-American literature selection (*Roll of Thunder, Hear My Cry* or *The Secret of Gumbo Grove*).

3. Students should then discuss their webs with their small groups and develop a group web to share with the class. These group webs should be completed on large chart paper or overheads, if possible, so that the class may see and discuss them. Have one member of each group share the group web with the class.

4. Display the different webs in the classroom, and discuss as a class the similarities and differences among the Group A webs and the Group B webs. Ask students to comment on any common themes they recognize between the two books.

5. Continue discussion of the books, using the following questions as a guide.

Reasoning Questions

▼ *Not only do different cultures have special customs and traditions, they also may perceive the world differently. How does this statement apply to the book you just read?*

▼ *Literature from all cultures employs strong characters to tell a story. What characters from your reading impressed you? Why? Give specific evidence from the book to support your opinion.*

▼ *What inferences can you make about what the characters learned in the book? On what evidence do you base your conclusions?*

▼ *What predictions might you make about the life of your favorite character after the story ends? What data from the books can you provide to support your predictions?*

▼ *Why does the author use a particular cultural group as the context for the story? What purposes does he or she have in doing so?*

▼ *How do the issues in the book relate to problems of society today? What are the implications of these problems for us/you?*

Change Question

▼ *What elements of change are evident in the book you read? How do they support our generalizations on change?*

6. Have students return to their small groups to discuss their written responses to the questions on the **Independent Reading Assignment** (Handouts 1C and 1D, from Lesson 1). Have students complete the section of the **Cultures and Change Matrix** (Handouts 7B and 7C) that applies to the African-American readings.

HOMEWORK

Read Book Three from the **Independent Reading Assignment** (Handouts 1C and 1D) in preparation for a discussion in Lesson 15.

EXTENSIONS

1. Read the literature selection which was assigned to the other group for this lesson. Compare the two books.

2. Find more books by the author of the book you read. Read several of these books and prepare book reviews about them, with a brief synopsis of the life of the author.

PERSUASION

Literature Web
(Handout 10A)

NAME: _____ DATE: _____

Key Words

Feelings

Reading

Ideas

Images or Symbols

Structure

LESSON
11

Introduction to Unit Research Project

CURRICULUM ALIGNMENT CODE

GOAL 1	GOAL 2	GOAL 3	GOAL 4	GOAL 5	GOAL 6
X	X			X	

INSTRUCTIONAL PURPOSE

▼ To analyze persuasive essays.

▼ To develop skills in working with sources and note-taking.

▼ To introduce the research model.

▼ To begin the unit research project.

MATERIALS USED

1. Need to Know Board (Handout 11A)

2. Characteristics of an Issue (Handout 11B)

3. Essays on Censorship: "Libraries Should Reflect Majority Values" by Phyllis Schlafly and "Libraries Should Reflect Diverse Views" by the American Library Association

4. Working with Sources (Handout 11C)

5. Standards of Reasoning (Handout 8C)

6. Developing an Issue (Handout 11D)

7. Research Model (Handout 11E)

ACTIVITIES

1. Ask students to discuss the meaning of the term *censorship* and how it might apply to libraries in schools and communities. Present the following problem to students:

   You are an editor for one of the newspapers in your city. Censorship in school libraries has become an issue in the upcoming school board election, and you plan to do a series of articles on censorship. The paper wants to consider all sides of the issue so that voters can make an informed choice among candidates for the school board. One candidate says that free access to information and literature is an essential ingredient for knowledge and freedom. Another candidate says that censorship is sometimes necessary to protect values, culture, and national security. The other school board candidates have not stated their viewpoints. As the editor you are required to research the issue, take a stand, and write an editorial. In addition, you must make a presentation to the Press Club to defend your point of view.

2. Use the **Need to Know Board** (Handout 11A) as a tool to help students begin brainstorming and discussing the problem. Present each of the board's three questions to students:

   ▼ *What do we know?*

   ▼ *What do we need to know?*

   ▼ *How can we find out?*

Have students respond to each of the questions. Then have them state why the information they give is important and what ideas they are pursuing with the questions they ask. Sample responses to the three questions are listed below.

A. Possible responses: What do we know?

   ▼ editor of newspaper

   ▼ one candidate says free access to information and literature are essential ingredients for knowledge and freedom

   ▼ one candidate says censorship is sometimes necessary to protect values, culture, and national security

   ▼ must write an editorial

   ▼ must defend position in a speech

B. Possible responses: What do we need to know?

   ▼ what does free access to information mean?

   ▼ are there other censorship issues?

   ▼ what are some examples of censorship?

   ▼ how has freedom been affected by censorship?

   ▼ what are the opinions of people in various communities about the issue?

C. Possible responses: How are we going to find out?

   ▼ research

   ▼ write advocacy groups

▼ read and evaluate some books

▼ review books for young people that have been banned

▼ interview librarians

3. Have students use their **Need to Know Board** to write a statement of the problem on a note card. Have students share their statements in pairs, revise as necessary to clarify the statements, and then attach the note cards to their **Need to Know Boards** for reference throughout the project.

4. Explain to students that the issue of censorship is one which has led to discussion in many communities. Share with students the following **Characteristics of an Issue** (Handout 11B):

▼ *The issue is a real world problem.*

▼ *The issue has stakeholders who may win or lose something, and they have differing points of view. (Multiple points of view surround the issue with groups standing to win or lose.)*

▼ *The issue is researchable. (Evidence can be found to support different points of view.)*

▼ *The issue is important enough for someone to spend time researching it.*

Discuss the difference between a topic (such as "penguins") and an issue (such as "Should hunting of penguins be forbidden by law?"). Ask how the issue of censorship of library books matches the criteria.

5. Distribute **Working with Sources** (Handout 11C) and discuss. Have students read one of the two essays on censorship and take notes, using the handout as a guide. Discuss the process and the essay as a class. Then have students read the second essay and work with a partner to discuss the second essay. As a class, discuss the points of view expressed in the two essays. Have students use the **Standards of Reasoning** (Handout 8C) to evaluate the two essays. Have them update their **Need to Know Board** with any additional information or questions.

6. Distribute copies of **Developing an Issue** (Handout 11D). Have students work in groups to identify the stakeholder groups for the issue of censorship. Have students then state their own point of view on the issue.

7. Have students use their stated point of view to write a persuasive paragraph on the issue. After students have written their paragraphs, have them exchange papers with a partner and critique one another's work, using the Hamburger Model and the **Standards of Reasoning**.

8. Point out to students that the essays they have read are only a sample of the many articles that are available on the subject of censorship. Emphasize that research on an issue should take students beyond merely summarizing known facts in a report or other product. Students should take and support a personal point of view in their role as editor of the city newspaper. Various perspectives may be surveyed in library materials, but primary resources such as interviews or polls may also contribute greatly. Introduce the **Research Model** (Handout 11E) that will serve as a guide in this process. Talk students through the model. Reassure them that you will revisit the model with them throughout the process to help them. (Note that students have already begun working on parts 1 and 2.)

9. Each student will develop a persuasive editorial and speech defending his or her point of view on the issue. Discuss with students the research assignment and the due dates on the two projects (a rough draft of the essay should be prepared by Lesson 20; the essay and speech are due in Lesson 22). Work with students on **setting goals for the project and developing a plan for achieving those goals**.

10. Introduce students to the **Research Center**. This Learning Center may include a regular and an electronic encyclopedia, nonfiction books, and other resources which will help students investigate their issue. A list of guiding questions and key terms to investigate may help students in their research efforts. In addition, this Center may include nonfiction materials about the authors whose works are included in the unit as well as the people, places, and things described in the readings, so that students may pursue areas of interest.

NOTES TO TEACHER

1. *More extended lessons and applications of the research process have been developed and published in* A Guide to Teaching Research Skills and Strategies in Grades 4–12, *available from the Center for Gifted Education at the College of William and Mary.*

2. *Censorship revolves around issues of values, choices, and control. Some parents feel that these issues are inappropriate for the classroom. In addition, examples of censored materials may be brought to class during the research work of the unit, with the potential to generate real and unwelcome censorship battles. You should be aware of how this issue might be received in your community and school and prepare the research lessons accordingly.*

3. *Numerous resources on the issue of censorship are available, including articles, books, annual book lists from the American Library Association, and web sites. Sample resources include the following:*

Beahm, G. (Ed.). (1993). *War of words: The censorship debate.* Kansas City, MO: Andrews and McMeel.

Public Agenda Foundation. (1987). *Freedom of speech: Where to draw the line.* Dayton, OH: Domestic Policy Association.

The New York Public Library. (1984). *Censorship: 500 years of conflict.* New York: Oxford University Press.

Censorship: For & against. (1971). New York: Hart.

Censorship: Opposing viewpoints. (1990). San Diego: Greenhaven.

Haight, A. L. (1978). *Banned books 387 B.C. to 1978 A.D.* New York: R. R. Bowker.

Doyle, R. P. (1991). *Banned books week '91: Celebrating the freedom to read.* Chicago, IL: American Library Association.
(This is a resource manual that is published annually.)

4. *Some examples of children's books that have been banned include the following:*

Steig, W. (1969). *Sylvester and the magic pebble.* New York: Simon and Schuster.
(All characters are animals. Police who are portrayed favorably happen to be presented as pigs.)

George, J. C. (1972). *Julie of the wolves.* New York: HarperCollins.
(The book was challenged because of its "socialist, communist, evolutionary, and anti-family themes.")

Paterson, K. (1977). *Bridge to Terabithia.* New York: Crowell.
(The book was challenged because it contains "profanity" including the phrase "Oh, Lord" and "Lord" used as an expletive.)

Seuss, Dr. (1971). *The Lorax.* New York: Random House.
(The book was challenged because it "criminalizes the foresting industry.")

HOMEWORK

1. Begin looking for resources that provide information on the censorship issue.

2. Finish a rough draft of your persuasive letter for the next lesson.

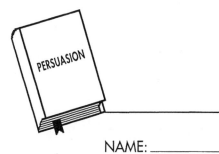

Need to Know Board

(Handout 11A)

NAME: _____ DATE: _____

What Do We Know?	What Do We Need to Know?	How Can We Find Out?

Characteristics of an Issue

(Handout 11B)

NAME: _____ DATE: _____

▼ **Real world.** An issue is a controversy or problem that people are discussing or should be discussing. It is ambiguous with no clear-cut or easy solutions. As new information is obtained, the problem changes.

▼ **Multiple points of view.** Different people or groups have different perspectives or points of view about an issue. Depending on how the issue is resolved, various groups and individuals (called stakeholders) stand to win or lose tangible things, such as income and recreational areas, or intangible things, such as solitude and freedom of speech.

▼ **Researchable with substantial information available.** Remember that to develop a convincing argument, you will need multiple sources of information and data. Important issues and real-world problems are informed by historical and contemporary information sources and by the collection and analysis of a variety of data.

▼ **Worthy topic and personal involvement.** Research offers the opportunity to ask questions about things that matter. While asking questions and seeking solutions, you have the chance to consider the arguments of others and to contribute your personal perspective and original thinking. When you care about an issue, you will be willing to spend time digging for evidence, taking a stand, developing an argument, and proposing a resolution to the problem.

Working with Sources

(Handout 11C)

NAME: _____ DATE: _____

1. Preview—Before you begin to read, a few steps will increase your understanding of the material.

    A. Look over the material and ask the following questions:

      ▼ *How long is this piece?*

      ▼ *What can I learn from the title?*

      ▼ *Do I know anything about the author?*

      ▼ *What do I know about the publisher?*

    B. Skim through the material as follows:

      ▼ *Find special features such as a summary, headings, tables or visual aids.*

      ▼ *Quickly read the first sentence of each paragraph if there is no summary or outline*

      ▼ *Scan the bibliography to check sources.*

2. Mark and make notes in the text—marking the text with a pencil rather than a highlighter allows you to make changes later and to make thoughtful notations.

    A. Use a pencil to mark important ideas—try underlining or putting a small check, exclamation point, or question mark in the margin.

    B. Reread the text and write notes in the margin. Write questions about things that puzzle you as you read, and list comments and big ideas.

3. Summarize with notes.

    A. Identify the topic sentence of each paragraph.

    B. Take notes that may include short quotations.

    C. Paraphrase or restate what you've read into your own words.

    D. Document your notes with full bibliographic information including page numbers.

Source: Miller, R. K. (1992). *The informed argument: A multidisciplinary reader and guide* (3d ed.). Fort Worth: Harcourt Brace Jovanovich, pp. 53–67.

4. Synthesize—relate one source to another.

  A. Ask yourself the following questions:

    ▼ *How does this material relate to whatever else I have already read on this topic?*

    ▼ *Does one source support another or conflict with it?*

    ▼ *How can I compare and contrast the sources?*

  B. Use your synthesis along with your own insights and research to write your persuasive essay on your issue.

Developing an Issue
(Handout 11D)

NAME: _____ DATE: _____

Developing an Issue

State the issue:

Identify the stakeholder groups:	Describe each group's position:

State your initial position:

Research Model
(Handout 11E)

NAME: _____ DATE: _____

---

1. **Identify your issue or problem.**

   What is the issue or problem?

   Who are the stakeholders and what are their positions?

   What is *your* position on this issue?

---

2. **Read about your issue and identify points of view or arguments through information sources.**

   What are my print sources?

   What are my media sources?

   What are my people sources?

   What are my preliminary findings based on a review of existing sources?

---

3. **Form a set of questions that can be answered by a specific set of data.**
   Examples:

   1. What would be the results of _____?

   2. Who would benefit and by how much?

   3. Who would be harmed and by how much?

   My research questions:

4. **Gather evidence through research techniques such as surveys, interviews, or experiments.**

   What survey questions should I ask?

   What interview questions should I ask?

   What experiments should I do?

5. **Manipulate and transform data so that it can be interpreted.**

   How can I summarize what I found?

   Should I develop charts, diagrams, or graphs to represent my data?

6. **Draw conclusions and make inferences.**

   What do the data mean? How can I interpret what I found out?

   How does the data support your original point of view?

   How does it support other points of view?

   What conclusions do you make about the issue?

7. **Determine implications and consequences.**

   What are the consequences of following the point of view that you support?

   Do I know enough or are there now new questions to be answered?

8. **Communicate your findings. (Prepare an oral presentation for classmates based on note cards and written report.)**

   What are my purpose, issue, and point of view, and how will I explain them?

   What data will I use to support my point of view?

   How will I conclude my presentation?

12

"The Pied Piper of Hamelin"

CURRICULUM ALIGNMENT CODE

GOAL 1	GOAL 2	GOAL 3	GOAL 4	GOAL 5	GOAL 6
X	X	X	X	X	X

INSTRUCTIONAL PURPOSE

▼ To develop analytical and interpretive skills in literature.

▼ To explore new vocabulary words.

▼ To explore music as a means of persuasion.

▼ To revise student writing.

MATERIALS USED

1. Music selections

2. "The Pied Piper of Hamelin" by Robert Browning

3. Literature Web (Handout 12A)

4. Vocabulary Web (Handout 12B)

5. Student Response Journals

6. Students' persuasive letters (Homework from Lesson 9)

7. Self-Assessment for Writing (Handout 12C)

8. Peer Assessment for Writing (Handout 12D)

9. Teacher Assessment for Writing (Handout 12E)

10. Standards of Reasoning (Handout 8C)

ACTIVITIES

1. Collect several short selections of music which were written with some sort of persuasive or motivational intent. Examples would include national anthems and other patriotic songs, marching songs, college fight songs and alma maters, songs for specific holidays, etc. Play several selections for students and ask them to write a sentence or two for each piece to describe how it made them feel or what thoughts it brought to their minds. Discuss student responses and their ideas about how music can be used to make an impression on people. Explain that in the poem they are about to read, music plays an important persuasive role.

2. Have students read "The Pied Piper of Hamelin" by Robert Browning and complete individual copies of a **Literature Web** (Handout 12A) about the poem. Have each student also select a short section of the poem to read aloud and read that section over carefully.

3. Divide students into small groups to share their webs. In their groups, students should also read their brief selections from the poem aloud and make a list of important things to remember when reading poetry aloud.

4. Discuss the webs as a class, then continue the discussion of the poem with the following questions:

Literary Response and Interpretation Questions

▼ *What was unusual about the Piper's appearance? What words would you use to describe him?*

▼ *How did the Piper persuade the Mayor to allow him to get rid of the rats? What evidence did the Piper use to support his argument?*

▼ *Why did the rats jump into the river?*

▼ *How did the solution to the original problem create new problems? How might the new problems have been avoided? What warning did the Piper provide that his power extended to more than just rats?*

▼ *What did the Piper mean by the words, "And folks who put me in a passion/ May find me pipe after another fashion"?*

▼ *Why do you think the Piper chose music to charm the rats and the children?*

▼ *Why do you think no one was able to stop the children? Did the children see the event as something positive or negative? How did the Mayor and Council perceive the event? How do you think the other townspeople felt?*

▼ *What title might you give to the Piper's song? Why? Does your title express the point of view of the Piper, the children, or the adults in the town? What titles might be given to the song by each of the other points of view?*

▼ *What is the lesson of the poem?*

Reasoning Questions

▼ *Was a thousand guilders a lot of money? Support your response with evidence from the poem.*

▼ *What evidence in the poem supports the idea that the Mayor and Council did not make wise use of the town's funds?*

▼ *What assumptions did the Mayor make about the Piper?*

▼ *What was the Piper's point of view about how he was treated? Were his actions justified? Why or why not?*

Change Questions

▼ *How did the society of Hamelin change after the events described in the poem? What efforts did the people of the town make to ensure that the events were remembered?*

▼ *How do the generalizations about change apply to this poem?*

▼ *How can music create changes in the ways people feel and act? Are these changes always positive? What are some examples of ways in which music may have affected events in history?*

5. Have students work in small groups to complete a **Vocabulary Web** (Handout 12B) for one of the following words from "The Pied Piper of Hamelin": ***vermin, subterranean, pied, piebald, pottage, paunch, mutinous, consternation***.

6. Give students the following sentence from the poem. Ask them to identify the part of speech of each underlined word and its function in the sentence. Provide time for students to ask questions about their independent grammar study.

   Once more he stept into the street; /And to his lips again/Laid his long pipe of smooth straight cane;

7. Have students respond to one of the following questions in their **Response Journals**:

   ▼ *Describe a time when you decided to be a follower of some person or idea.*

▼ *Describe a time when you chose to have someone else solve a problem for you and found that it only created more problems for you. What are some examples of problems you should solve on your own, and what are some problems that should be solved with help? How do you react to someone who helps you solve a problem?*

8. Have students take out their rough drafts of their persuasive letters (assigned in Lesson 9) for a revision workshop. Remind students of the following purposes of revision:

   ▼ *To clarify the writing; to figure out what you're trying to say.*

   ▼ *To identify audience reaction and needs; to fill in the gaps for your reader or to clarify your meaning.*

   ▼ *To ensure that the theme of your piece is maintained throughout.*

   ▼ *To refocus and restructure writing; to change the order or direction of your piece.*

   ▼ *To improve the quality of the piece of writing through changing paragraphs, sentences, and words.*

   Model the procedure of reading and revising by demonstrating with a short piece on the overhead projector. Use the **Assessments for Writing** (Handouts 12C, 12D, and 12E) to guide the discussion. Emphasize to students that as they work, they are focusing on revising for the purposes listed above and on the assessment form, not considering editing details such as spelling and punctuation. Remind them to pay attention to the central issue of the letter and to offer suggestions as to how the argument might need strengthening or additional reasons.

9. Have students independently complete a **Self-Assessment for Writing** (Handout 12C) for their persuasive letter. Then have students work in pairs to share their writing, using the **Peer Assessment for Writing** (Handout 12D) to guide the discussion. Encourage students to refer to the **Hamburger Model** and the **Standards of Reasoning** (Handout 8C) as they comment on one another's writing. Encourage students to offer one another positive comments about specific aspects of the writing, rather than "I like it" or something equally nonspecific, and to offer constructive suggestions for revision. Students may also conference with teachers on their writing assignment during this time, with reference to the **Teacher Assessment for Writing** (Handout 12E).

NOTE TO TEACHER

As examples of what is meant by revision, you might save some student examples to share with future classes. These should show substantial changes such as significant rewriting of paragraphs, additions of new ideas, deletions of old ideas, change in order and organization, etc. It is a common student misconception that revision means editing for mechanics.

HOMEWORK

Revise your persuasive letter, based on the discussions in class and the assessment forms.

EXTENSIONS

1. Find several picture book versions of the Pied Piper story and compare them. What aspects do they have in common? How are they different? Create your own picture book of the story.

2. Research the music of three different cultures. What similarities do you find across cultures?

3. Read *Peter Pan* by Sir J. M. Barrie. Compare Peter Pan to the Pied Piper.

Literature Web

(Handout 12A)

NAME: _____ DATE: _____

Key Words

Feelings

Reading

Ideas

Images or Symbols

Structure

PERSUASION

Vocabulary Web
(Handout 12B)

NAME: _____ DATE: _____

Synonyms:

Sentence:

Definition:

Antonyms:

Word:

Part of Speech:

Example:

Analysis

Word Families:

Stems:

Origin:

Self-Assessment for Writing
(Handout 12C)

NAME: _____ DATE: _____

ASSIGNMENT: _____

Directions: Grade your own writing. For each sentence below, circle the choice that describes your writing best.

1. My main idea is clear.	Needs Improvement	Satisfactory	Excellent
2. My details support the main idea.	Needs Improvement	Satisfactory	Excellent
3. My ideas flow smoothly and orderly.	Needs Improvement	Satisfactory	Excellent
4. The hamburger structure is clear (introduction, body, conclusion).	Needs Improvement	Satisfactory	Excellent
5. My vocabulary is rich and varied.	Needs Improvement	Satisfactory	Excellent

MY WRITING IS STRONG IN THESE WAYS:

_____

_____

_____

MY WRITING COULD BE IMPROVED IN THESE WAYS:

_____

_____

_____

Peer Assessment for Writing

(Handout 12D)

READER: _____ WRITER: _____

ASSIGNMENT: _____

Directions: Read your partner's writing sample carefully. For each sentence below, circle the choice that you think describes the writing.

1. The main idea is clear.	Needs Improvement	Satisfactory	Excellent
2. The details support the main idea.	Needs Improvement	Satisfactory	Excellent
3. The ideas flow smoothly and orderly.	Needs Improvement	Satisfactory	Excellent
4. The hamburger structure is clear (introduction, body, conclusion).	Needs Improvement	Satisfactory	Excellent
5. The vocabulary is rich and varied.	Needs Improvement	Satisfactory	Excellent

THE WRITING SAMPLE IS STRONG IN THESE WAYS:

_____

_____

_____

THE WRITING SAMPLE COULD BE IMPROVED IN THESE WAYS:

_____

_____

_____

Teacher Assessment for Writing
(Handout 12E)

STUDENT: _____ DATE: _____

ASSIGNMENT: _____

Directions: Circle the words that best describe the writing.

1. The main idea is clear.	Needs Improvement	Satisfactory	Excellent
2. Appropriate level of detail is provided to support main idea.	Needs Improvement	Satisfactory	Excellent
3. The ideas flow smoothly and orderly.	Needs Improvement	Satisfactory	Excellent
4. The hamburger structure is clear (introduction, body, conclusion).	Needs Improvement	Satisfactory	Excellent
5. The writing uses descriptive language and rich vocabulary.	Needs Improvement	Satisfactory	Excellent
Optional: Demonstrates correct grammar, usage, and mechanics.	Needs Improvement	Satisfactory	Excellent

PARTICULAR STRENGTHS:

_____

_____

AREAS NEEDING IMPROVEMENT:

_____

_____

LESSON

13

▼

Introduction to Debate

CURRICULUM ALIGNMENT CODE

GOAL 1	GOAL 2	GOAL 3	GOAL 4	GOAL 5	GOAL 6
	X		X	X	

INSTRUCTIONAL PURPOSE

▼ To develop skills in debate.

▼ To edit student writing.

MATERIALS USED

1. Debate Format (Handout 13A)
2. "The Pied Piper of Hamelin" by Robert Browning
3. Standards of Reasoning (Handout 8C)
4. Debate Evaluation Form (Handout 13B)
5. Revised Writing Assignment from Lesson 12
6. Editing (Handout 13C)

ACTIVITIES

1. Explain that persuasion can also be attempted in a formal way during a debate. Hand out the worksheet on **Debate Format** (Handout 13A) and use it to teach the skill of debating to students.

   ▼ *What is the difference between a debate and a discussion?*

   ▼ *What is the traditional set speaking order for a debate?*

   ▼ *How do you prepare for a debate?*

   ▼ *How are debates judged?*

2. Students will do a Practice Debate using an issue from "The Pied Piper of Hamelin." The debate topic is, **"Resolved: The mayor should have paid the Piper."**

3. Assign students to small groups as teams to be for or against the resolution. Allow students time to plan their arguments.

4. Using the procedure outlined in Handout 13A, have the teams debate. While the teams debate, the rest of the class critiques the debate using the **Debate Evaluation Form** (Handout 13B).

5. Discuss the debate.

6. Explain that students will be preparing for a debate on an issue that relates to censorship in the entertainment industry. The following are two suggestions:

   Resolved: That movie theaters must check age identification for young people who want to purchase tickets to PG-13 movies.

   Resolved: That warning labels should be placed on music CD's and cassettes that contain objectionable lyrics.

   Assign students to small groups of 2 or 3. They will prepare for the debate and present it in Lesson 17.

7. Have students respond to the following question in their **Response Journals**:

   ▼ *Assume that you have the ability to rid your town of its rats as easily as the Pied Piper did. Would you offer your services as a volunteer or would you ask for money? Explain.*

8. Distribute **Editing** (Handout 13C) and discuss with students the purposes and elements of editing. Have them work in pairs to edit the writing assignment from Lesson 12.

NOTES TO TEACHER

1. *Depending on the readiness level of your students, there are many levels of sophistication from which you can approach the debate activity. You may adjust the task demands and expectations accordingly.*

2. *For a more sophisticated approach than is outlined in this lesson, you may want to refer to the following article for more information on debate: Swicord, B. (1984). Debating with gifted fifth and sixth graders—Telling it like it was, is, and could be. Gifted Child Quarterly, 28, 127–129.*

3. *You should add more items to the list of issues that students will debate in Lesson 17 if you do not wish to have repetitions on the same topic. If your time is limited, you may have half of the class observe and critique one debate while the other half observes and critiques another at the same time.*

HOMEWORK

1. Prepare for a debate on one of the issues:

    Resolved: That movie theaters must check age identification for young people who want to purchase tickets to PG-13 movies.

    Resolved: That warning labels should be placed on music CD's and cassettes that contain objectionable lyrics.

    The debate will take place in Lesson 17.

2. Prepare a final copy of your persuasive letter. Send it to its intended recipient.

EXTENSIONS

1. Conduct an impromptu debate on whether you think "The Pied Piper" is a suitable story for young children.

2. Consider the expression "pay the piper" that is sometimes used in everyday speech.

    a) This is an example of a "literary allusion." Look up the term "allusion" and explain how it applies to this expression.

    b) Give an example of a sentence that might use this phrase.

3. Interview someone who debates competitively in high school or college. Find out the following:

    a) What format do they use for the debate?

    b) What are the scoring procedures they use?

    c) How do they prepare for the debate?

Debate Format

(Handout 13A)

NAME: _____ DATE: _____

What Is a Debate?

A debate is a series of formal spoken arguments for and against a definite proposal. The best solution is approved and adopted.

Debate is a special type of argument in which two or more speakers present opposing propositions in an attempt to win the audience to their sides. The teams are not concerned with convincing each other. The purpose is to try to alter the thinking of the audience by presenting the issues honestly with reliable evidence.

Why Debate?

Debate helps you develop skills in the following areas:

▼ Analyzing issues

▼ Backing up statements with proof

▼ Clearly expressing ideas

▼ Listening and tracking oral arguments

▼ Evaluating oral arguments

▼ Speaking extemporaneously

What Are the Rules of Debating?

Debates begin with a proposed solution to a problem. The proposal should begin with the word RESOLVED. Examples:

▼ Resolved: That animals should not be used in scientific experiments.

▼ Resolved: That the minimum age for getting a driver's license should be eighteen.

1. The affirmative team supports the proposition and the negative team opposes it. There are usually two members on each of the two teams.

2. Begin with careful research and analysis by both teams on the subject to be debated. Each member should know as much about the opponent's arguments as he does about his or her own position.

3. List the main arguments for both sides of the issue. Decide which arguments are worthy of being included and which are irrelevant and should be excluded. You might use the **Standards of Reasoning** (Handout 8C) to help strengthen the arguments. Find evidence that will prove the issue true or false (facts, examples, statistics, testimony, etc.).

4. Be prepared to answer the arguments of the other team's issues. Your answers make up what is called a REBUTTAL.

What Is the Format for a Debate?

Suggested Procedure:

First Affirmative Speech	3 minutes
First Negative Rebuttal	1.5 minutes
Second Negative Speech	3 minutes
Second Affirmative Rebuttal	1.5 minutes

The debate always begins and ends with the affirmative team.

Scoring will be done by giving the following:

▼ One point for each argument or two points for each argument with proof

▼ One point for each refutation of a reason

▼ Points for delivery (eye contact, expression, volume, body language, etc.) as follows:

Needs improvement	0 points
Satisfactory	1 point
Outstanding	2 points

Debate Evaluation Form
(Handout 13B)

TEAM MEMBERS: _____ DATE: _____

ISSUE: _____

FOR OR AGAINST? _____

Take notes while the debate is being presented. You might make tally marks in each category and complete the point count when the debate is over.

1. Reasons with no evidence provided (1 point each) _____

2. Reasons with evidence provided (2 points each) _____

3. Refutation of reasons given by opponents (1 point each) _____

4. Delivery (eye contact, body language, volume, expression, etc.): _____

        Needs improvement   0 points
        Satisfactory   1 point
        Outstanding   2 points

                                   TOTAL   _____

Comments:

Editing
(Handout 13C)

NAME: _____ DATE: _____

Editing your work is the polishing stage. You have the opportunity to use all that you know about vocabulary and grammar and learn even more from your classmates and teacher.

Proofreading

To get started on the editing process, you need to proofread. This is a different way of reading. Instead of reading for meaning, you should read word-for-word and look for errors. It is a very slow type of reading. In fact, one recommended method for careful proofreading is to read backwards so that you will be forced to look at each word.

Correcting Errors

Mark each error as you find it. Use a dictionary, a writing handbook, or the assistance of a friend to correct your work. You may want to ask your teacher for help with the final editing.

Common Errors to Look For

Use this list as a guide for things to check in your writing:

Spelling

Punctuation

Paragraph indentation

Capitalization of proper nouns

Subject and verb agreement

Consistent tense usage

Pronoun agreement

A Word to the Wise

Never turn in a finished piece of writing until you have proofread it very carefully. If the piece is very important, have someone else proofread it also.

LESSON
14

"I Have a Dream"

CURRICULUM ALIGNMENT CODE

GOAL 1	GOAL 2	GOAL 3	GOAL 4	GOAL 5	GOAL 6
X	X	X	X	X	X

INSTRUCTIONAL PURPOSE

▼ To analyze persuasive language in literature.

▼ To explore new vocabulary words.

MATERIALS USED

1. Video of the "I Have a Dream" speech, by Dr. Martin Luther King, Jr.

2. Text of the "I Have a Dream" speech, by Dr. Martin Luther King, Jr.

3. The Language of Persuasion (Handout 9C)

4. Vocabulary Web (Handout 14A)

ACTIVITIES

1. Give students some background in preparation for watching the video of Dr. Martin Luther King, Jr.'s March on Washington Address ("I Have a Dream"). On August 28, 1963, more than 200,000 people gathered in Washington, D.C. in a peaceful demonstration on behalf of equal justice for all. This speech was given by Dr. King from the steps of the Lincoln Memorial. His words, "I have a dream," quickly became symbolic of the goals of the civil rights movement.

2. Show the video and then have students use the written text of the speech as a reference for the rest of the lesson. Ask the following questions as part of a follow-up discussion:

   ▼ *What issues did Martin Luther King, Jr. talk about in his speech?*

▼ *Consider the sentence, "We have also come to this hallowed spot to remind America of the fierce urgency of now." What does King mean by the phrase "this hallowed spot"? What does he mean by the phrase "the fierce urgency of now"?*

▼ *What perspectives did people have on those issues in the 1960s? What is your evidence?*

▼ *How have those perspectives changed since the 1960s?*

3. Explore and analyze some of the uses of language in persuasion by asking students to identify a few examples of persuasive language in the speech. Remind students about **The Language of Persuasion** (Handout 9C). The following are some questions that may help in the process:

A. **Word choice**

▼ *Why does King use the word "dream" to appeal to his listeners? Why is it an effective word?*

B. **Figurative language**

▼ *Track the use of money allusions in King's speech. Why is the idea of "giving the Negro people a bad check" an effective metaphor?*

▼ *What other metaphors does King use and why are they effective?*

C. **Sentence patterns**

▼ *Repetition is a powerful tool in this speech. Cite examples and comment on how it ads to the appeal of the speech.*

D. **Imitative language patterns**

▼ *The opening line of King's speech is imitating the opening of another famous speech. Can you identify that speech?*

▼ *To what does the paragraph that starts, "I have a dream that one day every valley shall be exalted . . ." refer?*

E. **Concrete and abstract images**

▼ *King uses concrete images in connection with abstract ideas. For example, he talks about "freedom" with the image of a bell. What other concrete images does he use to illustrate concepts?*

4. Ask students to reread the speech and to mark all the examples of persuasive language they can find. Make a list of student findings and discuss.

5. Discuss historical trends in language by asking the following question:

▼ *If Martin Luther King, Jr. gave the "I Have a Dream" speech today, what elements of the language would likely be different and why?*

6. Have students complete a **Vocabulary Web** using one or more of the following words: ***proclamation, manacle, segregation, redemptive.***

7. Have students respond to the following question in their **Response Journals**:

▼ *If you could experience the "I Have a Dream" speech in only one form, would you prefer the videotape or the written text? Support your point of view.*

NOTE TO TEACHER

The text provided of King's speech is a transcription of the speech as it was delivered. Other, slightly different versions of the speech have also been published in written form. A possible extension for students would be to compare versions and analyze the reasons for any differences.

HOMEWORK

Finish the Hispanic-American selection from the independent reading assignment from Lesson 1 and the corresponding response writing in preparation for the next lesson.

PERSUASION

Vocabulary Web
(Handout 14A)

NAME: _____ DATE: _____

Synonyms:

Sentence:

Definition:

Antonyms:

Word:

Part of Speech:

Example:

Analysis

Word Families:

Stems:

Origin:

LESSON

15

▼

Discussion of Hispanic-American Literature

CURRICULUM ALIGNMENT CODE

GOAL 1	GOAL 2	GOAL 3	GOAL 4	GOAL 5	GOAL 6
X				X	X

INSTRUCTIONAL PURPOSE

▼ To develop analytical and interpretive skills in literature.

▼ To develop interviewing skills.

MATERIALS USED

1. *Going Home* by Nicholasa Mohr

2. *Taking Sides* by Gary Soto

3. Literature Web (Handout 15A)

4. Independent Reading Assignment (Handouts 1C and 1D, from Lesson 1) and students' written responses

5. Cultures and Change Matrix (Handouts 7B and 7C)

6. Need to Know Board (Handout 11A)

7. Interview Planning Sheet (Handout 15B)

ACTIVITIES

1. Divide students according to Group A and Group B (based upon **Independent Reading Assignments** from Lesson 1). Within each group, have students form smaller groups of 4–5 people.

2. Ask each student to complete a **Literature Web** (Handout 15A) independently, based on their reading of an Asian-American literature selection (*Going Home* or *Taking Sides)*.

3. Students should then discuss their webs with their small groups and develop a group web to share with the class. These group webs should be completed on large chart paper or overheads, if possible, so that the class may see and discuss them. Have one member of each group share the group web with the class.

4. Display the different webs in the classroom, and discuss as a class the similarities and differences among the Group A webs and the Group B webs. Ask students to comment on any common themes they recognize between the two books.

5. Continue discussion of the books, using the following questions as a guide.

Reasoning Questions

▼ *Not only do different cultures have special customs and traditions, they also may perceive the world differently. How does this statement apply to the book you just read?*

▼ *Literature from all cultures employs strong characters to tell a story. What characters from your reading impressed you? Why? Give specific evidence from the book to support your opinion.*

▼ *What inferences can you make about what the characters learned in the book? On what evidence do you base your conclusions?*

▼ *What predictions might you make about the life of your favorite character after the story ends? What data from the books can you provide to support your predictions?*

▼ *Why does the author use a particular cultural group as the context for the story? What purposes does he or she have in doing so?*

▼ *How do the issues in the book relate to problems of society today? What are the implications of these problems for us/you?*

Change Question

▼ *What elements of change are evident in the book you read? How do they support our generalizations on change?*

6. Have students return to their small groups to discuss their written responses to the questions on the **Independent Reading Assignment** (Handouts 1C and 1D, from Lesson 1). Distribute the **Cultures and Change Matrix** (Handouts 7B and 7C) and have students complete the section of the chart that applies to the Hispanic-American readings.

7. As a continuation of the research project, have students work in small groups to share information they have gathered on the censorship issue. Have them update their **Need to Know Boards** (Handout 11A) as a framework for discussion.

8. Discuss with students the idea of interviewing as a way to get information on the censorship issue. Have students brainstorm individuals they might want to interview. Discuss the **Interview Planning Sheet** (Handout 15B) as preparation for an interview. Discuss the importance of practicing for the interview and sending a thank-you note to the interviewee.

9. Remind students that they will complete a written editorial and a persuasive speech on their censorship issue. Students should have completed a rough draft of their editorial in time for Lesson 20.

HOMEWORK

Read Book Four from the **Independent Reading Assignment** (Handouts 1C and 1D) in preparation for a discussion in Lesson 20.

EXTENSIONS

1. Read the literature selection which was assigned to the other group for this lesson. Compare the two books.

2. Find more books by the author of the book you read. Read several of these books and prepare book reviews about them, with a brief synopsis of the life of the author.

Literature Web
(Handout 15A)

NAME: _____ DATE: _____

Key Words

Feelings

Reading

Ideas

Images or
Symbols

Structure

Interview Planning Sheet
(Handout 15B)

NAME: _____ DATE: _____

Name of person you are interviewing:

Why do you want to interview this person?

What do you want to tell this person about your issue?

What questions do you want to ask?

For example, to get started:

▼ What is the interviewee's perspective on the issue?

▼ How does the issue relate to the interviewee's life or work?

▼ What sources would the interviewee consult if she were in your position?

Other questions you want to ask:

LESSON
16
▼

"The Case for Public Schools"

CURRICULUM ALIGNMENT CODE

GOAL 1	GOAL 2	GOAL 3	GOAL 4	GOAL 5	GOAL 6
X	X	X	X	X	

INSTRUCTIONAL PURPOSE

▼ To develop analytical and interpretive skills in literature.

▼ To apply standards of reasoning.

▼ To explore new vocabulary words.

MATERIALS USED

1. "The Case for Public Schools" by Horace Mann

2. Standards of Reasoning (Handout 8C)

3. The Language of Persuasion (Handout 9C)

4. Vocabulary Web (Handout 16A)

ACTIVITIES

1. Provide students with some resources on the history of education in the United States. Have them work in small groups to create a timeline of the major events and figures in the development of public education in this country.

2. Have students read "The Case for Public Schools," an excerpt from Horace Mann's last report to the Massachusetts Board of Education in 1848. Ask students to work in small groups to identify the *issue* and the *point of view* expressed in the report.

3. Have students generate a list of the major reasons Mann presents in support of public schools. List the reasons on the board and discuss. Use the **Standards of Reasoning** (Handout 8C) to evaluate the reasons. Ask students whether they think Mann's argument is convincing or not and why.

4. Analyze the speech, using **The Language of Persuasion** (Handout 9C), the **Elements of Reasoning**, and the questions below.

A. **Word choice**

▼ *What does Mann mean by the words, "education creates or develops new treasures—treasures not before possessed or dreamed of by any one"? Why does he emphasize the word **treasure**?*

▼ *Find the places in the report in which Mann refers to the benefits which will be gained from universal education. According to Mann, who will benefit? Does he emphasize the benefits to the working classes or to the society as a whole? Why do you think he places the emphasis where he does?*

B. **Figurative language**

▼ *Why does Mann use the extended metaphor of the savage who learns to build a boat? What are the implications of this metaphor for education?*

▼ *What does Mann use as a comparison to a government who would "suffer its laboring classes to grow up without knowledge"? Is his comparison valid? Why or why not?*

C. **Sentence patterns**

▼ *Mann uses the words "wealth" and "wealthy" frequently in the report. Of what kind of wealth does he speak?*

D. **Imitative language patterns**

▼ *Find the references Mann makes to concepts of economics throughout the report. Why does he make these references? What inferences can you make about Mann's audience based on these references?*

E. **Concrete and abstract images**

▼ *What is meant by the words, "Education, then, beyond all other devices of human origin, is the great equalizer of the conditions of men—the balance-wheel of the social machinery"? Why does Mann try to create images of balance and equality?*

5. Have students work in small groups to complete a **Vocabulary Web** (Handout 16A) for one of the following words: *feudalism, factitious, prerogative, inestimable.*

6. Ask students to imagine that they were present when the report was given to the Massachusetts Board of Education. Tell them to select one part of the report that they found particularly effective or persuasive or one part with which they would argue. Have students prepare a one-minute speech to respond to their chosen parts of Mann's report. The speeches should be prepared based on the Hamburger Model, with an opening that expresses the student's point of view about the section of the report, several reasons supporting the point of view, and a conclusion. Have students write notes for their speeches on note cards and present their speeches to the class.

7. Have students respond to the following question in their **Response Journals**:

   ▼ *What treasures do you think education creates? What treasures have you found as a result of your education?*

HOMEWORK

Finish your preparations for the debate in the next lesson.

EXTENSIONS

1. Find out more about Horace Mann and his influence on American education. Who have been some other influential figures in the history of American education?

2. Write a description of what you think an ideal school would be like.

Vocabulary Web
(Handout 16A)

NAME: _____ DATE: _____

Synonyms:

Sentence:

Definition:

Antonyms:

Word:

Part of Speech:

Example:

Analysis

Word Families:

Stems:

Origin:

181

17

Debate Presentations

CURRICULUM ALIGNMENT CODE

GOAL 1	GOAL 2	GOAL 3	GOAL 4	GOAL 5	GOAL 6
	X		X	X	

INSTRUCTIONAL PURPOSE

▼ To debate issues.

▼ To evaluate debate presentations based on standards of reasoning and debate format.

MATERIALS USED

1. Debate Format (Handout 13A)

2. Stop watch

3. Debate Evaluation Form (Handout 17A)

4. Standards of Reasoning

5. Student Response Journals

ACTIVITIES

1. Begin the class with two teams debating the issues that were assigned in Lesson 13:

   Resolved: That movie theaters must check age identification for young people who want to purchase tickets to PG-13 movies.

   Resolved: That warning labels should be placed on music CD's and cassettes that contain objectionable lyrics.

2. Review the rules for debating (Handout 13A). One student should be the time keeper. Teams not debating are the score keepers to encourage listening skills.

3. Score the debate using the Debate Evaluation Form (Handout 17A) and discuss the debates. Have students refer to the **Standards of Reasoning** (Handout 8C) as they discuss the arguments that were presented in the debates.

4. Have students respond to the following questions in their **Response Journals**:

> ▼ *How did the arguments of the various teams affect your thinking about the issues? Did you change your mind about anything? How did the experience of doing a debate change your ideas about persuasion?*

HOMEWORK

1. Continue collecting examples of advertising for Lesson 19.

2. Continue your independent reading assignment for Lesson 20.

EXTENSION

Choose another topic to research and debate for more practice.

Debate Evaluation Form

(Handout 17A)

TEAM MEMBERS: _____ DATE: _____

ISSUE: _____

FOR OR AGAINST?_____

Take notes while the debate is being presented. You might make tally marks in each category and complete the point count when the debate is over.

1. Reasons with no evidence provided (1 point each)　　　　　　　_____

2. Reasons with evidence provided (2 points each)　　　　　　　_____

3. Refutation of reasons given by opponents (1 point each)　　　　_____

4. Delivery (eye contact, body language, volume, expression, etc.):　_____

        Needs improvement　　　　0 points
        Satisfactory　　　　　　　1 point
        Outstanding　　　　　　　2 points

                                TOTAL　　　_____

Comments:

LESSON
18
▼

"The Velvet Hangover"

CURRICULUM ALIGNMENT CODE

GOAL 1	GOAL 2	GOAL 3	GOAL 4	GOAL 5	GOAL 6
X	X	X	X	X	X

INSTRUCTIONAL PURPOSE

▼ To develop reasoning and interpretive skills in literature.

▼ To recognize elements of persuasion in a speech.

▼ To explore new vocabulary words.

MATERIALS USED

1. "The Velvet Hangover" by Václav Havel

2. Literature Web (Handout 18A)

3. The Language of Persuasion (Handout 9C)

4. Vocabulary Web (Handout 18B)

ACTIVITIES

1. Share with students some background on the fall of the Communist system in the countries of eastern Europe. Explain that in Czechoslovakia, a series of mass demonstrations led to the resignation of the Communist party in power and the establishment of a noncommunist government; these events were referred to as the "velvet revolution" because of the bloodless and smooth transition. In a free election in June of 1990, the country elected Václav Havel President of the newly named Czech and Slovak Federal Republic. Havel, a well-known playwright, had also been a political activist in Czechoslovakia for many years, leading to his popularity and election.

2. Have students read "The Velvet Hangover," a speech given by Havel in July 1990 at the opening of the Salzburg Festival in Austria. Have students work in small groups to complete a **Literature Web** (Handout 18A) about the speech.

3. Discuss the webs as a class, then continue discussion of the speech, using the following questions as a guide.

Literary Response and Interpretation Questions

▼ *What is the main idea or theme of Havel's speech? What ideas is he trying to express?*

▼ *What does Havel mean by the words, "the poetry was over and the prose was beginning; the country fair had ended and everyday reality was back"?*

▼ *Why was fear a part of the let-down feeling Havel experienced?*

▼ *Explain Havel's words, "history got in my way." Can you think of other examples in history or in your own life when unexpected events have forced plans to be changed?*

▼ *Have you ever had an experience similar to Havel's in which initial happiness over having achieved a goal changed to fear? Describe it.*

▼ *Why does Havel believe that it is more important than ever to get rid of fear of truth?*

▼ *How does Havel's discussion of fear relate to censorship?*

▼ *What does Havel mean by the words, "Perhaps hopelessness is the very soil that nourishes human hope"?*

Reasoning Questions

▼ *List some of the points Havel makes about the concept of fear. What does he mean when he says that "fear is not only a destructive condition"?*

▼ *What are the major issues Havel is trying to address in the speech? Of what is he trying to persuade people?*

▼ *What are the consequences for Havel's country of establishing a new government? What new issues will people have to face?*

▼ *What evidence of the effects of fear does Havel use to explain his feelings?*

▼ *How was persuasion important in the change of government in Czechoslovakia?*

Change Questions

▼ *What does Havel mean when he says, "We were very good at being persecuted and at losing. That may be why we are so flustered by our victories and so disconcerted that no one is persecuting us"? In what ways did his entire way of looking at the world have to change as a result of the revolution?*

▼ *What change is Havel trying to persuade his audience to make?*

▼ *How do the generalizations about change apply to this speech? What generalizations might you make about changes in government based on the speech?*

4. Have students refer to **The Language of Persuasion** (Handout 9C) to discuss the language of the speech. Use the questions below as a guide.

A. **Word choice**

▼ *List some of the adjectives Havel uses to describe his feelings over the course of the speech. How does he use words to create contrasts? Which words are the most effective, in your opinion, and why?*

▼ *Havel says that he has spoken in "an unstatesmanlike manner about my moments of hopelessness." Do you agree or disagree that his speech was unstatesmanlike? What effects do you think his speech had upon his listeners? Would you consider him more or less a leader after hearing his words?*

B. **Figurative language**

▼ *Havel makes many comparisons about the situation he now faces in helping to establish a new government. Which of the analogies seems most effective to you? Why?*

C. **Sentence patterns**

▼ *Why does Havel use the word "fear" as many times as he does? Read aloud a paragraph in which he uses the word many times. How does reading the paragraph aloud change the effects it has on the listener?*

D. **Imitative language patterns**

▼ *One of Franklin Delano Roosevelt's most famous speeches included the words, "We have nothing to fear but fear itself." What evidence is there in Havel's speech that he was aware of these words and wanted people to think of Roosevelt's words as they considered Havel's?*

▼ *In Greek mythology, Sisyphus was a cruel king who, after he died, was condemned to try to roll a huge boulder up a hill. Each time he neared the top, the boulder would roll back down and Sisyphus would have to start again. Why does Havel compare his situation to what Sisyphus would feel if he ever reached the top? How does reference to Greek mythology strengthen Havel's speech?*

E. **Concrete and abstract images**

▼ *What generalizations does Havel make about the historical role of people in eastern Europe? How does he see that role changing? In what ways is he trying to encourage people to change?*

5. Have students return to the webs and notes they completed about the Declaration of Independence in Lesson 9. Ask them to compare the two works, both of which form part of the history of revolutions. Have students compare the two pieces based upon the **Elements of Reasoning** (Handout 8A). Ask questions such as the following:

   ▼ *How were the purposes of the two works alike? How were they different?*

   ▼ *How might Havel's speech have been different if it had referred to a violent conflict such as the American Revolution rather than the bloodless change of power in Czechoslovakia?*

   ▼ *Which piece relied more heavily on specific data and evidence? Why? How is the choice of data to use related to the purpose of the document?*

   ▼ *How do the concepts of freedom and justice apply to both pieces?*

   ▼ *In what ways were both pieces persuasive messages intended to inspire courage?*

   ▼ *The Declaration of Independence was intended to be shared in written form; Havel's speech was delivered orally. How do the texts of the two pieces reflect the way they were to be shared?*

6. Have students work in small groups to complete a **Vocabulary Web** (Handout 18B) for one of the following words from "The Velvet Hangover": ***totalitarian, paradox, catastrophe, august, ubiquitous, egocentrism***.

7. Ask students to respond to the following question in their **Response Journals**:

   ▼ *Describe a time when you felt let down after a major event—when "the poetry was over and the prose was beginning." How did you handle the let-down feelings?*

HOMEWORK

Finish collecting your examples of advertisements for the next lesson.

EXTENSIONS

1. Read Greek and Roman myths such as that of Sisyphus in Hamilton's *Mythology* (1942), *The Greek Way* (1942) or *The Roman Way* (1932).

2. Compile a chart, such as the one below, of allusions to myths that you encounter in literature and daily life. For instance, what is the relationship of the products Mercury (a car) and Ajax (a cleanser) to the characters for whom they are named?

Allusions to Myths

Name or Word	Definition or Identification	Current or Literary Use	Implication for Persuasion
Sisyphus	Cruel king of Corinth condemned to roll stone up hill in Hades only to have it roll back down	Havel's speech	Vivid, convincing image of difficult job unexpectedly completed
Mercury	Roman god—messenger to other gods—wings on feet	Car name	
Ajax			

191

PERSUASION

Literature Web
(Handout 18A)

NAME: _____ DATE: _____

Key Words

Feelings

Reading

Ideas

Images or Symbols

Structure

193

PERSUASION

Vocabulary Web
(Handout 18B)

NAME: _____ DATE: _____

Synonyms:

Sentence:

Definition:

Antonyms:

Word:

Part of Speech:

Example:

Analysis

Word Families:

Stems:

Origin:

LESSON

19

▼

Advertising

CURRICULUM ALIGNMENT CODE

GOAL 1	GOAL 2	GOAL 3	GOAL 4	GOAL 5	GOAL 6
	X		X	X	

INSTRUCTIONAL PURPOSE

▼ To examine elements of persuasion in advertising.

▼ To apply techniques of persuasion in creating an advertisement.

MATERIALS USED

1. Examples of advertisements collected by students

2. Student Response Journals

ACTIVITIES

1. In small groups, have students share the examples of advertising that they were assigned to collect in Lesson 6. Have them categorize the ads based on techniques of persuasion that are used in the ads. They should make a list of the techniques of persuasion that they are able to identify.

2. Discuss the techniques of persuasion that students have identified. Make a master list with examples noted.

3. In small groups, have students create an ad for the extermination services of the Pied Piper. They may use any format including print ads, radio ads, TV ads, Internet ads, junk mail brochures, and billboards.

4. Have students share their ads. The rest of the class should identify the techniques of persuasion that are used in each of the student ads.

5. Have students think of examples of jingles that are used in advertising such as soft drinks, bandages, and bologna. Discuss the effectiveness of these jingles in persuading the listener to buy the product.

    ▼ *Who is targeted as a potential buyer of this product?*

    ▼ *What is the purpose of each of the jingle ads?*

    ▼ *Does the jingle format have any powers of persuasion that are different from other forms of advertising?*

    ▼ *How effective is each of the jingles?*

6. Have students respond to the following in their **Response Journals**:

    ▼ *When have you been persuaded to want something because of an advertisement? If you bought it, did it live up to the claims of the ads?*

HOMEWORK

1. Finish reading Book Four from the Independent Reading Assignment, and complete the writing responses. It is due for Lesson 20.

2. Finish a rough draft of your editorial on your research issue and notes for your speech.

EXTENSIONS

1. Interview someone who works in the field of advertising. Find out what techniques of persuasion they use as tools of the trade. Are there any that you did not identify in your study of the examples of ads?

2. Make a word bank of advertising words such as "slogan" or "jingle."

3. Find out what restrictions are imposed on certain areas of the advertising industry. For example, cigarettes may not be advertised on TV. How does this relate to the issue of book censorship that you are researching?

20

Discussion of Native American Literature

CURRICULUM ALIGNMENT CODE

GOAL 1	GOAL 2	GOAL 3	GOAL 4	GOAL 5	GOAL 6
X				X	X

INSTRUCTIONAL PURPOSE

▼ To develop analytical and interpretive skills in literature.

▼ To revise student writing.

▼ To prepare for research presentation.

MATERIALS USED

1. *Morning Star, Black Sun: The Northern Cheyenne Indians and America's Energy Crisis* by Brent Ashabranner

2. *Rising Voices: Writings of Young Native Americans* by Arlene Hirschfelder & Beverly Singer

3. Literature Web (Handout 20A)

4. Independent Reading Assignment (Handouts 1C and 1D from Lesson 1) and students' written responses

5. Cultures and Change Matrix (Handouts 7B and 7C)

6. Self-Assessment for Writing (Handout 20B)

7. Peer Assessment for Writing (Handout 20C)

8. Teacher Assessment for Writing (Handout 20D)

9. Standards of Reasoning (Handout 8C)

ACTIVITIES

1. Divide students according to Group A and Group B (based upon **Independent Reading Assignments** from Lesson 1). Within each group, have students form smaller groups of 4–5 people.

2. Ask each student to complete a **Literature Web** (Handout 20A) independently, based on their reading of an Native American literature selection (*Morning Star, Black Sun* and *Rising Voices*).

3. Students should then discuss their webs with their small groups and develop a group web to share with the class. These group webs should be completed on large chart paper or overheads, if possible, so that the class may see and discuss them. Have one member of each group share the group web with the class.

4. Display the different webs in the classroom, and discuss as a class the similarities and differences among the Group A webs and the Group B webs. Ask students to comment on any common themes they recognize between the two books.

5. Continue discussion of the books, using the following questions as a guide.

Reasoning Questions

▼ *Not only do different cultures have special customs and traditions, they also may perceive the world differently. How does this statement apply to the book you just read?*

▼ *Literature from all cultures employs strong characters to tell a story. What characters from your reading impressed you? Why? Give specific evidence from the book to support your opinion.*

▼ *What inferences can you make about what the characters learned in the book? On what evidence do you base your conclusions?*

▼ *What predictions might you make about the life of your favorite character after the story ends? What data from the books can you provide to support your predictions?*

▼ *Why does the author use a particular cultural group as the context for the story? What purposes does he or she have in doing so?*

▼ *How do the issues in the book relate to problems of society today? What are the implications of these problems for us/you?*

Change Question

▼ *What elements of change are evident in the book you read? How do they support our generalizations on change?*

6. Have students return to their small groups to discuss their written responses to the questions on the **Independent Reading Assignment** (Handouts 1C and 1D, from Lesson 1). Distribute the **Cultures and Change Matrix** (Handouts 7B and 7C) and have students complete the section of the chart which applies to the Native American readings.

7. Have students complete a **Self-Assessment for Writing** (Handout 20B) for their persuasive editorial on the research topic. Have them work in small groups to read one another's essays and use the **Peer Assessment for Writing** (Handout 20C) to make comments and guide discussion. They should also consider the **Standards for Reasoning** (Handout 8C) as they evaluate the essays. Students may also conference with the teacher during this time, using the **Teacher Assessment for Writing** (Handout 20D). Students should use the comments gained from their peers and their teacher to begin final revision on their research essays.

8. Provide time for students to practice and ask questions about their oral presentations on their research topic.

HOMEWORK

1. Finish revisions on your research essay and speech and have them prepared for Lesson 22.

2. Read *The Valiant*.

EXTENSIONS

1. Read the literature selection which was assigned to the other group for this lesson. Compare the two books.

2. Find more books by the author of the book you read. Read several of these books and prepare book reviews about them, with a brief synopsis of the life of the author.

Literature Web

(Handout 20A)

NAME: _____ DATE: _____

Key Words

Feelings

Reading

Ideas

Images or
Symbols

Structure

Self-Assessment for Writing

(Handout 20B)

NAME: _____ DATE: _____

ASSIGNMENT: _____

Directions: Grade your own writing. For each sentence below, circle the choice that describes your writing best.

1. My main idea is clear.	Needs Improvement	Satisfactory	Excellent
2. My details support the main idea.	Needs Improvement	Satisfactory	Excellent
3. My ideas flow smoothly and orderly.	Needs Improvement	Satisfactory	Excellent
4. The hamburger structure is clear (introduction, body, conclusion).	Needs Improvement	Satisfactory	Excellent
5. My vocabulary is rich and varied.	Needs Improvement	Satisfactory	Excellent

MY WRITING IS STRONG IN THESE WAYS:

_____

_____

_____

MY WRITING COULD BE IMPROVED IN THESE WAYS:

_____

_____

_____

Peer Assessment for Writing

(Handout 20C)

READER: _____ WRITER: _____

ASSIGNMENT: _____

Directions: Read your partner's writing sample carefully. For each sentence below, circle the choice that you think describes the writing.

1. The main idea is clear.	Needs Improvement	Satisfactory	Excellent
2. The details support the main idea.	Needs Improvement	Satisfactory	Excellent
3. The ideas flow smoothly and orderly.	Needs Improvement	Satisfactory	Excellent
4. The hamburger structure is clear (introduction, body, conclusion).	Needs Improvement	Satisfactory	Excellent
5. The vocabulary is rich and varied.	Needs Improvement	Satisfactory	Excellent

THE WRITING SAMPLE IS STRONG IN THESE WAYS:

_____

_____

_____

THE WRITING SAMPLE COULD BE IMPROVED IN THESE WAYS:

_____

_____

_____

Teacher Assessment for Writing
(Handout 20D)

STUDENT: _____ DATE: _____

ASSIGNMENT: _____

Directions: Circle the words that best describe the writing.

1. The main idea is clear.	Needs Improvement	Satisfactory	Excellent
2. Appropriate level of detail is provided to support the main idea.	Needs Improvement	Satisfactory	Excellent
3. The ideas flow smoothly and orderly.	Needs Improvement	Satisfactory	Excellent
4. The hamburger structure is clear (introduction, body, conclusion).	Needs Improvement	Satisfactory	Excellent
5. The writing uses descriptive language and rich vocabulary.	Needs Improvement	Satisfactory	Excellent

Optional:

Demonstrates correct grammar, usage, and mechanics.	Needs Improvement	Satisfactory	Excellent

PARTICULAR STRENGTHS:

_____

_____

AREAS NEEDING IMPROVEMENT:

_____

_____

LESSON

21

The Valiant

CURRICULUM ALIGNMENT CODE

GOAL 1	GOAL 2	GOAL 3	GOAL 4	GOAL 5	GOAL 6
X		X		X	X

INSTRUCTIONAL PURPOSE

▼ To develop analytical and interpretive skills in literature.

▼ To compare reading a play to reading short stories.

▼ To explore new vocabulary words.

MATERIALS USED

1. *The Valiant* by Holworthy Hall and Robert Middlemass

2. Literature Web (Handout 21A)

3. Vocabulary Web (Handout 21B)

4. Student Response Journals

ACTIVITIES

1. Students will have read the play *The Valiant* prior to the class meeting (homework from Lesson 20). Ask them to complete a **Literature Web** (Handout 21A) about the play to focus their ideas. Have them share their webs in small groups, then discuss as a class.

2. Continue discussion of the play, using the following questions as a guide.

Literary Response and Interpretation Questions

▼ *The Warden and Father Daly feel differently about Dyke than they do about other prisoners. Why?*

▼ *Much of what we know about the characters comes from the stage directions. What qualities are we told about each of the characters? What additional characteristics should an actor add? Stage the scene*

211

between Dyke and the girl. Have students act out the roles of Dyke, the girl, the Warden, and Father Daly.

▼ *If you had been Dyke's attorney, what arguments would you have given to try to get him a reduced sentence?*

▼ *What does Dyke mean when he says, ". . . the whole story and both sides of it, which you never heard and never will—and they never heard it in the courtroom, either"? Why did he not tell his side of the story in the courtroom?*

▼ *Why does the Warden say of Dyke, "This boy never heard of Shakespeare—much less learned him"? What evidence is there earlier in the play that Dyke is a well-read man?*

▼ *What qualities does Dyke reveal about himself in the meeting with the girl?*

▼ *Why does Dyke tell the story about Joseph Anthony Paris's actions in the war? What purpose does the story serve?*

▼ *What do you think Dyke would have done with the bonds if the girl had not come?*

▼ *What is meant by the words, "Cowards die many times before their death; The valiant never taste of death but once"? Why does Dyke continue to say these words?*

Reasoning Questions

▼ *How does the concept of courage apply to this story? Does Dyke display more or less courage by withholding the truth of his identity from the Warden and Father Daly? From the girl? Would the girl have been more or less comforted if he had said he was her brother?*

▼ *What evidence can you find that supports the view that the girl is Dyke's sister? What evidence supports the view that she is not his sister?*

▼ *What assumptions did the Warden make about the girl before she arrived? Why was he surprised at her appearance?*

▼ *What inferences can you make about Dyke's character, based on evidence in the story?*

▼ *How does the concept of justice apply to the story?*

Change Questions

▼ *Describe the various changes in Dyke's actions during the conversation with the girl. What decisions did he make during the scene?*

> ▼ *If Dyke had admitted to being Joseph Paris, how would the last part of the play have changed? Would the end have been easier or more difficult for him? How would the girl's image of her brother have changed?*

> ▼ *How does the play support the generalizations about change?*

3. As a class, make a Venn diagram comparing reading a play to reading a short story. Make another Venn diagram comparing reading a play to seeing one performed. Ask students how the stage directions influenced their understanding of the play.

4. Have students work in small groups to complete a **Vocabulary Web** (Handout 21B) for one of the following words from *The Valiant*: **valiant, felonious, malice, martyr, autobiography, sovereign, metropolitan, insouciant, indulgent, dubiously, vacuity.**

5. Present students with the following sentence from the play. Have them identify the part of speech of each word and its function in the sentence. Provide time for students to ask questions about their independent grammar study, and remind them that their grammar packet should be completed in time for a post-assessment in the next lesson.

    Goodnight, goodnight! <u>Parting</u> *is such* <u>sweet</u> *sorrow that I* <u>shall say</u> *goodnight til it be* <u>morrow</u>.

6. Have students respond to the following in their **Response Journals**:

> ▼ *The girl tells the Warden that the uncertainty has made her mother sick. The mother would rather hear some bad news than remain unsure of her son's whereabouts. Would you rather hear bad news than be uncertain about something? Write a short paper giving reasons why you would prefer bad news, or uncertainty. Try to recall a personal experience which you can use to support your position.*

NOTES TO TEACHER

1. *If possible, students should be given the opportunity to attend a live performance of a play. A play which would be suitable for high-ability students at this level should be read and discussed, followed by attendance at a performance and a subsequent discussion and critique. If this scenario is possible, it may be done in place of this lesson and discussion. If attendance at a play is not possible, then the reading and discussion of* The Valiant *should take place.*

2. *The reading of this play provides the opportunity for an in-depth discussion of the issue of capital punishment. If students raise this issue, it should be addressed; however, because of the sensitivity of the topic, teachers should carefully consider whether to raise the question for open discussion. An extension activity in which students debate the topic or act as a jury for the character in the play might be a helpful way to frame discussion of the issue.*

HOMEWORK

1. Finish your research editorial, and practice your speech for a presentation in the next lesson.

2. Finish your grammar self-study packet. There will be a post-assessment for grammar in the next lesson.

EXTENSIONS

1. Do a Readers' Theater performance of *The Valiant*.

2. In your judgment, is the main purpose of prison to punish prisoners, to rehabilitate them, or a combination of the two? Argue in a short paper your belief on this issue.

3. Read the play *Twelve Angry Men*, by Reginald Rose. Write a short paper about the role of prejudice in the initial reactions of many of the jurors. Watch the movie of the same name and discuss how the actors' performances compare to your impressions from reading the play.

4. Suppose that Dyke left a note in his cell before the girl came to visit him. The note told the Warden what to do with the Liberty Bonds. What would it say? Write the note that Dyke might have left.

PERSUASION

Literature Web
(Handout 21A)

NAME: _____ DATE: _____

Key Words

Feelings

Reading

Ideas

Images or
Symbols

Structure

215

Vocabulary Web

(Handout 21B)

NAME: _____ DATE: _____

Synonyms:

Sentence:

Definition:

Antonyms:

Word:

Part of Speech:

Example:

Analysis

Word Families:

Stems:

Origin:

LESSON
22

Research Presentation

CURRICULUM ALIGNMENT CODE

GOAL 1	GOAL 2	GOAL 3	GOAL 4	GOAL 5	GOAL 6
	X	X	X	X	

INSTRUCTIONAL PURPOSE

▼ To present research on the issue of censorship.

▼ To enhance oral presentation skills.

▼ To use standards of reasoning to assess oral argument.

▼ To assess grammar skills.

MATERIALS USED

1. Oral Presentation Evaluation Form (Handout 22A)

2. Standards of Reasoning (Handout 8C)

3. Student research projects

4. Student Response Journals

5. Post-Assessment for Grammar (included in Section III)

ACTIVITIES

1. Review characteristics of a good oral presentation, using the **Oral Presentation Evaluation Form** (Handout 22A) as a basis for the discussion. Discuss the **Standards of Reasoning** (Handout 8C) as key aspects of evaluating arguments.

2. Have students consider the original research problem, presented in Lesson 11. Remind students that they are now to present their persuasive speeches as though they are the editor of the city paper speaking to the Press Club. Have students give their presentations. Invite the listeners of each speech to ask questions in their role as Press Club attendees. Have students use the evaluation forms to assess their own work and that of their peers.

219

3. After speeches have been given, discuss areas of strength and suggestions for improvement. Have students turn in their persuasive editorials.

4. Have students respond to the following questions in their **Response Journals**:

   ▼ *How have your views on censorship changed as a result of doing this project?*

5. Distribute the **Post-Assessment for Grammar** (from Section III) and have students complete.

NOTE TO TEACHER

It may be helpful to videotape student presentations and watch them again later to allow students to critique their own work.

HOMEWORK

1. Complete your **Cultures and Change Matrix** (Handout 7B or 7C) for the next lesson.

2. If you have not yet written thank-you notes to your interviewees for your research project, complete the notes for homework.

Oral Presentation Evaluation Form

(Handout 22A)

SPEAKER: _____ DATE: _____

ASSIGNMENT: _____

Directions: Circle the choice that best describes each of the following.

ORGANIZATION

1. The purpose of the presentation was clear.	Needs Improvement	Satisfactory	Excellent
2. The speaker included effective examples.	Needs Improvement	Satisfactory	Excellent
3. The speaker showed knowledge of the subject.	Needs Improvement	Satisfactory	Excellent
4. The presentation closed with a strong, interesting idea that restated the purpose.	Needs Improvement	Satisfactory	Excellent

DELIVERY

1. The speaker made frequent eye contact with the audience.	Needs Improvement	Satisfactory	Excellent
2. The presentation was loud enough.	Needs Improvement	Satisfactory	Excellent
3. The speaker's words were clear enough to be understood.	Needs Improvement	Satisfactory	Excellent

THE BEST PART OF THIS PRESENTATION WAS:

_____

_____

A SUGGESTION FOR IMPROVEMENT IS:

_____

_____

LESSON
23

▼

Closing Discussion on the Concept of Change

CURRICULUM ALIGNMENT CODE

GOAL 1	GOAL 2	GOAL 3	GOAL 4	GOAL 5	GOAL 6
X	X			X	X

INSTRUCTIONAL PURPOSE

▼ To assess student understanding of the generalizations about change.

▼ To develop persuasive writing skills.

MATERIALS USED

1. Cultures and Change Matrix (Handouts 7B and 7C)

2. Final Writing Assignment (Handout 23A)

3. Student Response Journals

ACTIVITIES

1. Divide students into small groups within their reading divisions from the **Independent Reading Assignment** (from Lesson 1). Have students share their **Cultures and Change Matrix** (Handouts 7B and 7C) within their small groups and complete a combined chart of their ideas to share with the class. Share and discuss the combined charts. Have students compare the different charts within each reading division and look for similarities across the two larger groups. Ask students to consider the importance of change as a concept across all the readings.

2. Have students use the **Cultures and Change Matrix** and their notes from other unit readings and assignments to help them in a discussion synthesizing unit learning. Guide the discussion with questions such as those listed below:

- ▼ *What elements of change are reflected across cultures? How does a person's cultural identity influence an understanding about change?*

- ▼ *Give an example of a character from one of the readings who demonstrated remarkable change. How would you have described the character at the beginning? At the end? How would you describe the change which took place?*

- ▼ *Give an example of a reading from the unit which demonstrated a major social change. What factors were influential in the change?*

- ▼ *In many books, individual change and cultural change parallel each other. What examples of this can you give from your reading?*

- ▼ *What role does individual perception play in judgments we make about change?*

- ▼ *How does the idea of persuasion relate to the changes in the unit readings? In which instances was persuasion especially influential in a change?*

- ▼ *How did you change as you read the literature pieces? Which one was most important to you? Which characters did you feel especially close to?*

- ▼ *If you had to persuade a character in one of the literature pieces to make a change in his or her life, who would it be, what would be the change, and how would you persuade them to make it?*

3. Revisit the five generalizations about change, discussing examples of how the ideas about change were illustrated in the literature of the unit.

- ▼ Change is linked to time.
- ▼ Change may be positive or negative.
- ▼ Change may be perceived as orderly or random.
- ▼ Change is everywhere.
- ▼ Change may happen naturally or may be caused by people.

4. Divide students into five small groups. Assign each group one of the change generalizations. Allow 10–15 minutes of discussion within the groups to address the following question as it relates to that generalization. Students should take notes on the discussion.

- ▼ *How have the literature pieces of this unit supported the generalization?*

5. Have students share their findings in a whole class discussion.

6. Discuss with students how their understanding of persuasion has grown and changed over the course of the unit. Review some of the examples and techniques of persuasion which have been studied. Distribute copies of the **Final Writing Assignment** (Handout 23A) and discuss the assignment. Students are to write an essay supporting the statement, "People may cause change through the use of persuasion." Encourage students to consider both positive and negative changes which resulted from persuasion as they develop their arguments. They should use specific examples from the literature of the unit to support their argument, and they may use their **Cultures and Change Matrix**, their **Response Journals**, and other notes and writing from the unit to assist them in developing their essays.

7. Have students re-read their written products from the unit and respond to the following question in their **Response Journals**:

   ▼ *How have your written products changed during the unit?*

NOTE TO TEACHER

The writing assignment given in this lesson serves a dual purpose. It may be used as an additional assessment of student persuasive writing skills, as well as providing a closing unit assessment on the concept of change.

HOMEWORK

Complete the Final Writing Assignment. Revise and edit your essay carefully before writing a final copy.

Final Writing Assignment

(Handout 23A)

NAME: _____ DATE: _____

Write a persuasive essay using the Hamburger Model to support the following statement:

People may cause change through the use of persuasion.

Use specific examples from the literature and activities of the unit to support your argument. Consider both positive and negative changes that have been caused by persuasion. Check your essay against the Standards of Reasoning to evaluate the strength of your reasons and how well they are explained. Make sure your essay has a strong conclusion.

LESSON

24

Post-Assessment of Literature Interpretation and Persuasive Writing

CURRICULUM ALIGNMENT CODE

GOAL 1	GOAL 2	GOAL 3	GOAL 4	GOAL 5	GOAL 6
X	X			X	X

INSTRUCTIONAL PURPOSE

- ▼ To develop reasoning and interpretive skills in literature.

- ▼ To administer the unit post-assessments in literature interpretation and persuasive writing.

- ▼ To assess student progress on unit goals.

MATERIALS USED

1. "Stopping by Woods on a Snowy Evening" by Robert Frost

2. Post-Assessment for Literature (Handout 24A)

3. Literature Interpretation Scoring Rubric for Pre- and Post-Assessments and Examples

4. Post-Assessment for Writing (Handout 24B)

5. Persuasive Writing Scoring Rubric for Pre- and Post-Assessments and Examples

6. Overall Student Assessment Report (Handout 24C)

ACTIVITIES

1. Have students read the poem "Stopping by Woods on a Snowy Evening" and take the **Post-Assessment for Literature** (Handout 24A).

2. Have students keep their papers and the poem and discuss the post-assessment questions. Guide the discussion further with questions such as the following:

Literary Response and Interpretation Questions

▼ *Why does the speaker stop to watch the woods? Why would the horse think that to be strange? What is the difference between what the horse would want and what the speaker wants?*

▼ *What kind of snowstorm is illustrated in the poem? What words tell you about the atmosphere of the evening?*

▼ *Read the line, "The woods are lovely, dark and deep." How would the meaning of the line be different if there were a comma after the word "dark"?*

▼ *How are the structure and rhyme scheme of the last stanza different from those of the other stanzas?*

▼ *Why does the poet repeat the line, "And miles to go before I sleep"?*

Reasoning Questions

▼ *What inferences might you make about the owner of the woods? On what evidence do you base your inferences?*

▼ *How does the concept of responsibility apply to the poem?*

Change Questions

▼ *How do the generalizations about change apply to the poem?*

▼ *What feelings might a reader get from the isolated phrase, "The darkest evening of the year"? How does the rest of the poem change or dispel those feelings?*

3. Collect the **Post-Assessment for Literature**.

4. Distribute the **Post-Assessment for Writing** (Handout 24B). Have students complete the post-assessment, then discuss the question and students' responses. After the discussion, collect the papers.

NOTES TO TEACHER

1. *Compare individual assessment papers to each student's pre-assessment papers for literature and for writing to give you a basis for citing improvement that has taken place. Comparing scores alone may not adequately or definitively reflect the changes that have occurred. The rubrics included with the lesson may be used to provide the basis for scoring student responses.*

2. *Use the **Overall Student Assessment Report** (Handout 24C) to rate student progress on each goal from participation in the unit.*

Post-Assessment for Literature
(Handout 24A)

NAME: _____ DATE: _____

1. State an important idea of the poem in a sentence or two.

2. Use your own words to describe what you think the poet means by the words, "But I have promises to keep, And miles to go before I sleep."

3. What does the poem tell us about the idea of change? Support what you say with details from the poem.

4. Create a different title for this poem. Give two reasons from the poem for your new title.

Literature Interpretation Scoring Rubric for Pre- and Post-Assessments

1. **State an important idea of the reading in a sentence or two.**

Score	Description of Response
1	limited, vague, inaccurate, confusing, only quotes from reading
2	simplistic, literal statement; uses only part of main idea; creates title rather than main idea
3	insightful, addresses theme

2. **Use your own words to describe what you think the author means by . . .**

Score	Description of Response
1	limited, vague, inaccurate; rewording only
2	accurate but literal response
3	insightful, interpretive response

3. **What does the poem tell us about the idea of change? Support what you say with details from the poem.**

Score	Description of Response
1	limited, vague, inaccurate; only quotes from story
2	valid generalization without support **or** well-supported example
3	valid generalization about change is made and well supported

4. **Create a title for this poem. Give two reasons from the poem for your new title.**

Score	Description of Response
1	limited, vague, or title given without reasons
2	appropriate but literal response; at least one reason given
3	insightful, meaningful title given with support

Sample Student Responses
Post-Assessment for Literature

1. **State an important idea of the reading in a sentence or two.**

   SAMPLE 1-POINT RESPONSE:

   - *He's afraid to walk through the woods because the person who owns them might see him and arrest him for trespassing.*

   SAMPLE 2-POINT RESPONSE:

   - *It's about a man who's watching the woods in a snowstorm because he thinks it's really beautiful, but then he has to go somewhere so he can't stay in the woods.*

   SAMPLE 3-POINT RESPONSE:

   - *Sometimes it's important to stop and look at beautiful things in the world, but you also can't forget about your responsibilities.*

2. **Use your own words to describe what you think the author means by . . .**

   SAMPLE 1-POINT RESPONSE:

   - *He made a promise to somebody that he would travel a certain number of miles.*

   SAMPLE 2-POINT RESPONSE:

   - *He probably has somebody waiting for him at home that he promised he would be home by a certain time, and he still has a ways to go.*

   SAMPLE 3-POINT RESPONSE:

   - *He has a long way to travel, either actually traveling or just doing things in life, and he can't just do what he wants to do all the time because other people are depending on him.*

3. **What does the poem tell us about the idea of change? Support with details.**

   SAMPLE 1-POINT RESPONSE:

   - *The change in the poem is that the man decides not to stay in the woods because his horse doesn't want to.*

   SAMPLE 2-POINT RESPONSE:

   - *The change in the poem happens when the man remembers that he has promises he has to keep and so he changes his mind about staying and watching the snow. He changes from doing what he wants to doing what he is supposed to do.*

SAMPLE 3-POINT RESPONSE:

- *This poem shows that change can happen naturally or be caused by people. The man in the poem is watching a nature change, which is that the woods are filling up with snow, and he thinks it's really beautiful. He can't stay and watch it, though, because he has things to do, so he causes a change himself when he leaves the woods and moves on.*

4. **Create a title for this poem. Give two reasons from the poem for your new title.**

SAMPLE 1-POINT RESPONSE:

- *The Confused Horse.*

SAMPLE 2-POINT RESPONSE:

- *Miles to Go. The man in the poem has a long way to go, and since he says that line two times it is a very important part of the poem.*

SAMPLE 3-POINT RESPONSE:

- *I would call it "A Pause on the Journey" because when he stops to watch the woods, he's just resting in the middle of his long trip, and lots of times you only notice beautiful things when you stop in the middle of everything else you're doing to look at them.*

Post-Assessment for Writing

(Handout 24B)

NAME: _____ DATE: _____

Directions: Write a paragraph to answer the question below. State your opinion, include three reasons for your opinion, and write a conclusion to your paragraph.

Do you think the poem, "Stopping by Woods on a Snowy Evening," should be required reading for all students in your grade?

Persuasive Writing Scoring Rubric for Pre- and Post-Assessments

Claim or Opinion

Score	Description of Response
0	No clear position exists on the writer's assertion, preference, or view, and context does not help clarify it.
2	Yes/no alone or writer's position is poorly formulated, but reader is reasonably sure what the paper is about because of context.
4	A basic topic sentence exists, and the reader is reasonably sure what the paper is about based on the strength of the topic sentence alone.
6	A very clear, concise position is given as a topic sentence, and the reader is very certain what the paper is about. Must include details such as grade level, title of the reading, or reference to "the story," etc.

Data or Supporting Points

Score	Description of Response
0	No data are offered that are relevant to the claim.
2	Scant data (one or two pieces) are offered, but what data exist are relevant to the claim.
4	At least three pieces of data are offered. They are relevant but not necessarily convincing or complete.
6	At least three pieces of accurate and convincing data are offered.

Warrant or Elaboration on Data

Score	Description of Response
0	No warrant or elaboration is offered.
2	An attempt is made to elaborate at least one element of the data.
4	More than one piece of data is explained, but the explanation is weak and lacks thoroughness, **or** one piece of data is well elaborated.
6	The writer explains more than one piece of data in such a way that it is clear how they support the argument. At least one piece of data is convincingly and completely elaborated.

(Adapted from N. Burkhalter, 1995)

Conclusion

Score	Description of Response
0	No conclusion/closing sentence is provided.
2	A conclusion/closing sentence is provided.

Sample Student Responses
Post-Assessment for Writing

Sample 1

Yes, because it's a beautiful poem that makes you think of a beautiful time of year. Also it's by a very famous poet. That's why I think you should read it.

Score: Claim = 2   Total Score = 8
       Data = 2
       Warrant = 2
       Conclusion = 2

Sample 2

No, the poem shouldn't be required. This poem is too easy for kids our age because it's short and the words are easy. Also kids can't relate to it because who travels on a horse anymore? I also don't think kids should have to read poems if they don't want to. Most kids like to read more exciting stuff with more of a plot like stories and longer books.

Score: Claim = 4   Total Score = 12
       Data = 4
       Warrant = 4
       Conclusion = 0

Sample 3

"Stopping by Woods on a Snowy Evening" should be required reading for all kids in my grade for a lot of reasons. First, it's a well-written poem that has good rhyme and a good meter. It would be a pretty poem to memorize and recite for your parents. Second, the poem was written by a famous American poet we should all know about. This is also one of his most famous poems, and lots of people will know what you're talking about if you say "And miles to go before I sleep," so it's a way to relate to people. My other reason is that the poem teaches kids two really good lessons. The first lesson is that sometimes you should stop being busy all the time and pay attention to the things in the world that are beautiful. The other lesson is that you can't do that all the time, though, because you have responsibilities and you can't let people down when you have promised them something. For all of those reasons, all the kids should be required to read this poem.

Score: Claim = 6   Total Score = 20
       Data = 6
       Warrant = 6
       Conclusion = 2

Overall Student Assessment Report

(Handout 24C)

NAME: _____ DATE: _____

Directions: Please rate each of the following using the scale: 3 = Excellent; 2 = Satisfactory; 1 = Needs Improvement. Also, write a brief narrative assessing the student's ability, progress, or other pertinent information.

	Needs Improvement	Satisfactory	Excellent
GOAL 1—INTERPRETATION OF LITERATURE			
—Pre-Assessment for literature	1	2	3
—Literature webs	1	2	3
—Quality of literature discussion	1	2	3
—Post-Assessment for literature	1	2	3
GOAL 2—WRITING			
—Pre-Assessment for writing	1	2	3
—Persuasive writing	1	2	3
—Literary response writings	1	2	3
—Persuasive letter	1	2	3
—Research editorial	1	2	3
—Post-Assessment for writing	1	2	3
GOAL 3—GRAMMAR/VOCABULARY			
—Grammar Pre-Assessment	1	2	3
—Vocabulary webs	1	2	3
—Grammar discussions	1	2	3
—Post-Assessment for grammar	1	2	3

	Needs Improvement	Satisfactory	Excellent
GOAL 4—LISTENING/SPEAKING			
—Small/large group discussion	1	2	3
—Persuasive speeches	1	2	3
—Debate	1	2	3
—Presentation of research	1	2	3
GOAL 5—REASONING			
—Issue charts	1	2	3
—Discussion/application of elements and standards of reasoning	1	2	3
GOAL 6—CHANGE			
—Cultures and Change Matrix	1	2	3
—Final writing assignment on change (Lesson 23)	1	2	3
MAJOR PROJECTS			
—Research project on significant issue	1	2	3
—Debate presentation	1	2	3

Briefly comment on the student's progress in understanding the concept of "change."

_____

_____

_____

Briefly comment on the student's progress in reasoning ability.

_____

_____

_____

SECTION

III

GRAMMAR STUDY

Inspecting Our Own Ideas: Student Grammar Study

by Michael C. Thompson

This section includes a packet of materials designed to be duplicated and distributed to students for independent or guided study of grammar. Also included are teacher instructions and a pre-assessment and post-assessment.

In classrooms where students have already completed the grammar packet during the course of a previous unit, the packet may be used as a resource. Students will continue to work on grammar by completing the grammar activities that are embedded in the lessons of the unit.

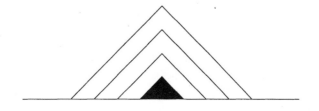

▼ Teacher Instructions

This grammar study, although it does explore numerous technical details of grammar, is not designed to teach technical details. Rather, the primary purpose of the study is to introduce students to the wonder and pleasure of grammar, an aspect of grammar that is usually missing from the commonly used, technically oriented studies of grammar.

In order to accomplish this deeper purpose, many of the facts and concepts of grammar must be mentioned, since in discussing the power of grammar we must give students some concrete sense of what grammar is, and some sense of how its elements operate to accomplish their deeper purposes.

But the object of attention, which I want to bring to sharpest focus in the middle of my lens, is that grammar is lovely, and exciting, and irresistible, and that it takes very little imagination to demonstrate these qualities. I am aware that popular misconceptions exist that grammar is an arid and uninteresting subject, but these are unenlightened and uninformed prejudices that are easily discarded, or in the case of the youngest students, easily prevented.

The goal of the study, therefore, is to create an enlightened enthusiasm for the study of ideas in language; it is not to construct a stern gauntlet of terms to be memorized. The goal is to bring students' attention to the most introspective and human aspects of grammar.

Accordingly, the process of study itself must be human, pleasant, and flexible. There is no strict series of assignments or procedures. The primary activity is for the student to read and to think. The role of the teacher is to act as an encouraging and appreciative mentor for the student, by studying the unit and viewing it in its best light, by introducing the grammar study to the student warmly and optimistically, by working closely with the student in frequent conversation to build comprehension and appreciation. All of this should be accomplished in a manner that I can only describe as more artistic than methodic.

As a practical procedure, look through the unit with the student, and agree upon an appropriate place to stop the first reading session, based on the length of time available in your own circumstances and on the student's abilities. Allow the student to read, think, and make notes if appropriate. When the student is ready, come together and talk, with as much mutual enjoyment as possible, about the elements of grammar included in the reading. Review any written exercises that the student has done. Then agree on the extent of the next reading, and continue in this fashion. It will be important, at the end of the unit, to have a summary conversation which extracts all of the best ideas that have been gained.

As a professional educator, you should not hesitate to use this study as a flexible resource that you can supplement with your own creativity; the only danger would be to bury the positive spirit of the unit in a well-intentioned but counterproductive series of technical exercises. There will be plenty of time for such activities in the students' lives. The purpose of this unit is grammar appreciation.

Assessments: Before you distribute the grammar packet to students, duplicate and administer the pre-assessment on the next two pages. An answer key follows the student assessment pages. After completion of the packet, administer the post-assessment to measure student growth in grammar.

Grammar Pre-Assessment

NAME: _____ DATE: _____

Fill in the blanks.

1. A group of words that has a subject and a predicate is called a(n) _____.

2. The noun or pronoun that the sentence is about is called the _____.

3. The part of the sentence that says something about the subject is called the _____.

4. How many kinds of words are there in our language? _____.

5. A word that names a person, place, or thing is called a(n) _____.

6. A word that modifies a noun or pronoun is called a(n) _____.

7. A word that shows action is called a(n) _____.

8. A word that joins two words into a pair is called a(n) _____.

9. A word that shows emotion is called a(n) _____.

10. A word group acting as a single part of speech is a(n) _____.

Underline the complete subjects of these sentences.

11. The engineer designed a building.

12. Leonardo painted a beautiful painting.

13. Yes, the boy and the girl became friends quickly.

14. The explorer Balboa discovered the Pacific Ocean.

15. Caesar and his Roman legions defeated the Gauls in France.

Circle the correct answer.

16. In the sentence "The engineer designed a building," the word *engineer* is a(n)

    a. noun   b. pronoun   c. adjective   d. adverb

17. In the sentence "The engineer designed a building," the word *designed* is a(n)

   a. noun   b. verb   c. adjective   d. adverb

18. In the sentence "The engineer designed a building," the word *a* is a(n)

   a. conjunction   b. adverb   c. preposition   d. adjective

19. In the sentence "Yes, the boy and the girl became friends quickly," the word *and* is a(n)

   a. conjunction   b. preposition   c. interjection   d. adverb

20. In the sentence "Yes, the boy and the girl became friends quickly," the word *yes* is a(n)

   a. conjunction   b. preposition   c. interjection   d. adverb

21. In the sentence "Yes, the boy and the girl became friends quickly," the word *quickly* is a(n)

   a. adjective   b. adverb   c. interjection   d. conjunction

22. In the sentence "Caesar and his Roman legions defeated the Gauls in France," the word *in* is a(n)

   a. conjunction   b. preposition   c. interjection   d. adverb

23. In the sentence "Caesar and his Roman legions defeated the Gauls in France," the word *defeated* is a(n)

   a. verb   b. conjunction   c. preposition   d. adverb

24. In the sentence "Leonardo painted a beautiful painting," the word *beautiful* is a(n)

   a. noun   b. verb   c. adjective   d. adverb

25. In the sentence "Leonardo painted a beautiful painting," the word *painting* is a(n)

   a. noun   b. verb   c. adjective   d. adverb

An extra challenge:

Explain, in your own words, why grammar is important.

Grammar Pre-Assessment
Answer Key

Fill in the blanks.

1. A group of words that has a subject and a predicate is called a <u>sentence</u>.

2. The noun or pronoun that the sentence is about is called the <u>subject</u>.

3. The part of the sentence that says something about the subject is called the <u>predicate</u>.

4. How many kinds of words are there in our language? <u>eight</u>

5. A word that names a person, place, or thing is called a <u>noun</u>.

6. A word that modifies a noun or pronoun is called an <u>adjective</u>.

7. A word that shows action is called a <u>verb</u>.

8. A word that joins two words into a pair is called a <u>conjunction</u>.

9. A word that shows emotion is called an <u>interjection</u>.

10. A word group acting as a single part of speech is a <u>phrase</u>.

Underline the complete subjects of these sentences.

11. <u>The engineer</u> designed a building.

12. <u>Leonardo</u> painted a beautiful painting.

13. Yes, <u>the boy and the girl</u> became friends quickly.

14. <u>The explorer Balboa</u> discovered the Pacific Ocean.

15. <u>Caesar and his Roman legions</u> defeated the Gauls in France.

Circle the correct answer.

16. In the sentence "The engineer designed a building," the word *engineer* is a(n)

    a. <u>noun</u>   b. pronoun   c. adjective   d. adverb

17. In the sentence "The engineer designed a building," the word *designed* is a(n)

    a. noun   b. <u>verb</u>   c. adjective   d. adverb

18. In the sentence "The engineer designed a building," the word *a* is a(n)

    a. conjunction   b. adverb   c. preposition   d. <u>adjective</u>

19. In the sentence "Yes, the boy and the girl became friends quickly," the word *and* is a(n)

    a. <u>conjunction</u>   b. preposition   c. interjection   d. adverb

20. In the sentence "Yes, the boy and the girl became friends quickly," the word *yes* is a(n)

    a. conjunction   b. preposition   c. <u>interjection</u>   d. adverb

21. In the sentence "Yes, the boy and the girl became friends quickly," the word *quickly* is a(n)

    a. adjective   b. <u>adverb</u>   c. interjection   d. conjunction

22. In the sentence "Caesar and his Roman legions defeated the Gauls in France," the word *in* is a(n)

    a. conjunction   b. <u>preposition</u>   c. interjection   d. adverb

23. In the sentence "Caesar and his Roman legions defeated the Gauls in France," the word *defeated* is a(n)

    a. <u>verb</u>   b. conjunction   c. preposition   d. adverb

24. In the sentence "Leonardo painted a beautiful painting," the word *beautiful* is a(n)

    a. noun   b. verb   c. <u>adjective</u>   d. adverb

25. In the sentence "Leonardo painted a beautiful painting," the word *painting* is a(n)

    a. <u>noun</u>   b. verb   c. adjective   d. adverb

An extra challenge:

Explain, in your own words, why grammar is important.

Grammar Post-Assessment

NAME: _____ DATE: _____

Fill in the blanks.

1. A group of words that has a subject and a predicate is called a(n) _____.

2. The noun or pronoun that the sentence is about is called the _____.

3. The part of the sentence that says something about the subject is called the _____.

4. How many kinds of words are there in our language? _____.

5. A word that names a person, place, or thing is called a(n) _____.

6. A word that modifies a noun or pronoun is called a(n) _____.

7. A word that shows action is called a(n) _____.

8. A word that joins two words into a pair is called a(n) _____.

9. A word that shows emotion is called a(n) _____.

10. A word group acting as a single part of speech is a(n) _____.

Underline the complete subjects of these sentences.

11. The mathematician solved a problem.

12. Raphael painted a beautiful mural.

13. Oh, the owl and the pussycat went to sea quickly.

14. The explorer Columbus discovered the New World.

15. Hannibal and his army defeated the Romans in Italy.

Circle the correct answer.

16. In the sentence "The mathematician solved a problem," the word *mathematician* is a(n)

    a. noun   b. pronoun   c. adjective   d. adverb

17. In the sentence "The mathematician solved a problem," the word *solved* is a(n)

    a. noun   b. verb   c. adjective   d. adverb

18. In the sentence "The mathematician solved a problem," the word *a* is a(n)

    a. conjunction   b. adverb   c. preposition   d. adjective

19. In the sentence "Oh, the owl and the pussycat went to sea quickly," the word *and* is a(n)

    a. conjunction   b. preposition   c. interjection   d. adverb

20. In the sentence "Oh, the owl and the pussycat went to sea quickly," the word *Oh* is a(n)

    a. conjunction   b. preposition   c. interjection   d. adverb

21. In the sentence "Oh, the owl and the pussycat went to sea quickly," the word *quickly* is a(n)

    a. adjective   b. adverb   c. interjection   d. conjunction

22. In the sentence "Hannibal and his army defeated the Romans in Italy," the word *in* is a(n)

    a. conjunction   b. preposition   c. interjection   d. adverb

23. In the sentence "Hannibal and his army defeated the Romans in Italy," the word *defeated* is a(n)

    a. verb   b. conjunction   c. preposition   d. adverb

24. In the sentence "Raphael painted a beautiful mural," the word *beautiful* is a(n)

    a. noun   b. verb   c. adjective   d. adverb

25. In the sentence "Raphael painted a beautiful mural," the word *mural* is a(n)

    a. noun   b. verb   c. adjective   d. adverb

An extra challenge:

Explain, in your own words, why grammar is important.

Grammar Post-Assessment
Answer Key

Fill in the blanks.

1. A group of words that has a subject and a predicate is called a <u>sentence</u>.

2. The noun or pronoun that the sentence is about is called the <u>subject</u>.

3. The part of the sentence that says something about the subject is called the <u>predicate</u>.

4. How many kinds of words are there in our language? <u>eight</u>

5. A word that names a person, place, or thing is called a <u>noun</u>.

6. A word that modifies a noun or pronoun is called an <u>adjective</u>.

7. A word that shows action is called a <u>verb</u>.

8. A word that joins two words into a pair is called a <u>conjunction</u>.

9. A word that shows emotion is called an <u>interjection</u>.

10. A word group acting as a single part of speech is a <u>phrase</u>.

Underline the complete subjects of these sentences.

11. <u>The mathematician</u> solved a problem.

12. <u>Raphael</u> painted a beautiful mural.

13. Oh, <u>the owl and the pussycat</u> went to sea quickly.

14. <u>The explorer Columbus</u> discovered the New World.

15. <u>Hannibal and his army</u> defeated the Romans in Italy.

Circle the correct answer.

16. In the sentence "The mathematician solved a problem," the word *mathematician* is a(n)

    a. <u>noun</u>   b. pronoun   c. adjective   d. adverb

17. In the sentence "The mathematician solved a problem," the word *solved* is a(n)

    a. noun   b. <u>verb</u>   c. adjective   d. adverb

18. In the sentence "The mathematician solved a problem," the word *a* is a(n)

    a. conjunction   b. adverb   c. preposition   d. <u>adjective</u>

19. In the sentence "Oh, the owl and the pussycat went to sea quickly," the word *and* is a(n)

    a. <u>conjunction</u>   b. preposition   c. interjection   d. adverb

20. In the sentence "Oh, the owl and the pussycat went to sea quickly," the word *Oh* is a(n)

    a. conjunction   b. preposition   c. <u>interjection</u>   d. adverb

21. In the sentence "Oh, the owl and the pussycat went to sea quickly," the word *quickly* is a(n)

    a. adjective   b. <u>adverb</u>   c. interjection   d. conjunction

22. In the sentence "Hannibal and his army defeated the Romans in Italy," the word *in* is a(n)

    a. conjunction   b. <u>preposition</u>   c. interjection   d. adverb

23. In the sentence "Hannibal and his army defeated the Romans in Italy," the word *defeated* is a(n)

    a. <u>verb</u>   b. conjunction   c. preposition   d. adverb

24. In the sentence "Raphael painted a beautiful mural," the word *beautiful* is a(n)

    a. noun   b. verb   c. <u>adjective</u>   d. adverb

25. In the sentence "Raphael painted a beautiful mural," the word *mural* is a(n)

    a. <u>noun</u>   b. verb   c. adjective   d. adverb

An extra challenge:

Explain, in your own words, why grammar is important.

▼ Inspecting Our Own Ideas: Student Grammar Study

by Michael C. Thompson

As you begin to read this short study of grammar and to think about the ideas you will find here, you should know that there is one important purpose for what you are doing. It is not to learn a large number of facts, or to memorize terms, or to score points. Lots of grammar books can help you learn facts and terms. This study is different. Its purpose is to show you the deeper meaning of grammar that is usually missing from the grammar fact books—the part that many people never understand.

What is this deeper meaning?

It is that grammar is a kind of magic lens, a secret thinking method we can use to peek inside our own minds and to detect the designs of our own ideas.

Using grammar this way, we can learn about ourselves, learn about what makes us human, learn about why some ideas are clear and others are confused, learn about beautiful ways to share our thoughts with other people.

In order to make the most of what you will read, you should understand from the beginning that, even though there will be facts and details to learn, the facts are not the point. The point is the point. And so as you read, do what the coaches always tell you: keep your eye on the ball.

Do not forget that you are concentrating on the deep thinking, the deep meaning, the ability to appreciate the real power of grammar.

The best way to do this is to begin by previewing the study with your teacher. Look over it together, and agree on how much you should read in your first session. Then go read, and think, and reread. Make notes on your ideas and on the questions you have that the reading doesn't answer. Then meet with your teacher to talk about what you have learned and to look over any of the written exercises you may have done. Keep working in this way until you have read the entire grammar study and can discuss it completely with your teacher or other students, depending upon your class situation.

Remember that grammar is a kind of higher order thinking, like logic or mathematics. Grammar can show us secrets that no other thinking method can show us. If you read and think carefully, you will never forget that grammar is a wonderful tool for the mind.

▼ 1. Ideas, Language, and Grammar

How do we talk to each other?

How do we write to each other?

How do we read what someone else has written?

We use **language**. Language is our way of putting words together to make our **ideas**.

Any time we use words to **say something about something**, that is an idea!

We have to **say something . . . about something**.

In other words, an idea is made of **two parts**. One part is **what we are talking about**, and the other part is **what we are saying about it**.

We might say something about ourselves. Or we might say something about an object, such as a distant spiral galaxy in deep space, or a glowing hologram, or a thundering Triceratops. We might say something about wispy, white, cirrostratus clouds in a blue, summer sky. If we did that, we might say. "Wispy, white, cirrostratus clouds in a blue, summer sky floated high over my head."

Do you see the two parts of that idea?

What we are talking about:

> Wispy, white, cirrostratus clouds in a blue, summer sky

What we are saying about it:

> floated high over my head.

In this idea, we are using words in language to make an idea about cirrostratus clouds.

Of course, if wispy, white clouds in a blue, summer sky floated high over our heads, there would probably be a bird—high, high up—flying near the cloud. This would be a strong bird indeed, since cirrostratus clouds are found at 20,000 feet and higher! There would probably be summer insects buzzing around, eating fresh leaves and drinking nectar from the flowers. The grass would probably be cool and feel good on our bare feet. It would be nice.

Let's get back to language and ideas. Another idea could be, "I'm nobody." In this idea, we are saying something about something. Part one: we are talking about ourself. Part two: what are we saying about ourself? That we are nobody. Of course, this idea comes from a very famous poem by Emily Dickinson, one of America's very greatest poets. And when she said "I'm nobody," she was using irony to change the meaning from bad to good! If you read the rest of the poem, you will see how quickly Emily Dickinson accomplishes this change of meaning.

So, ideas have two parts.

Guess what? We have a very special way to study ideas that we make out of words in language. This special way to study language is called **grammar**.

Grammar is a way of thinking about language.

Using grammar, we can inspect one of our own language ideas, and see how language is made! We can do lots of things with grammar. We can find an idea's two parts, and we can find all of the groups of words in the idea, and we can even look at each word by itself and see what it does to make the idea work. This helps us to understand ourselves, and to understand how we think! In the pages that follow, you will learn about grammar, and about how grammar helps us to understand our own ideas.

REVIEW: Let's look again at the ideas we have discussed. Think carefully about each of these points:

language: our way of putting words together to express our ideas
idea: a two-part thought about something
the two parts of an idea: what we are talking about, and what we are saying about it
grammar: a special way of thinking about language

▼ 2. Sentence—A Subject and Its Predicate

In grammar, we have a special word to describe an idea that is made of two parts. This special word is **sentence**. A sentence is an idea. We sometimes say that a sentence is a **complete thought**, but this is just a different way of saying the same thing—that a sentence is an idea.

Would you like to know an interesting fact? Our English word *sentence* comes from a very old word, *sententia*, which was a word used thousands of years ago in an ancient language called *Latin*. Latin was the language spoken by the ancient Romans of Italy. To the ancient Romans, the word *sententia* meant "way of thinking." Latin was also the source of our English word *cirrostratus*, which we saw in the first section of this discussion. The word *cirrostratus* comes from the Latin stems *cirrus*, meaning "curl," and *stratus*, meaning "layer." Cirrostratus clouds form a thin, "curly layer" of clouds. We will see that many of the words used in grammar have very logical meanings that are based on ancient Latin or Greek words.

Now, we learned that a sentence is an idea that is complete. But what makes a sentence's idea complete?

It is complete because it has both of the two parts that it needs to make sense to someone. Until it has both of these two important parts, it is not finished, not complete.

Let's think about this for a minute. If I wish to understand you, then there are two things that I need to know:

1. I need to know **what you are talking about**;

   and

2. I need to know **what you are saying about it**.

If I do know these two things, then I can understand you. If, however, I do not know what you are talking about, or if I do not know what you are saying about it, then I will not understand you.

Grammar gives us names for these two parts of the sentence. The first part of the sentence, what it is about, is called the **complete subject**. The second part of the sentence, what we are saying about the subject, is called the **complete predicate**. Let's look at some examples:

COMPLETE SUBJECT	COMPLETE PREDICATE
(What the idea is about)	(What we are saying about the subject)
The crane	fishes patiently in the lake.
They	would banish us.
The people	could fly.
Crick and Watson	discovered DNA.
I	loved my friend.
Lenny	is a boy in my class.
That day	was one of the coldest.
He	had several beds of zinnias.
She	had a little thin face.
I	am

Notice that a sentence does not have to be long. Sometimes a sentence only has two words in it. "Pterodactyls landed" is a sentence. Even though it is short, it has a subject, *Pterodactyls*, and a predicate, *landed*.

Do you know what pterodactyls were? They were flying dinosaurs that had wings of skin, and that became extinct at the end of the Mesozoic era. In Arizona fossil pterodactyls have been found that had 40-foot wingspans. They are called *pterodactyls* because they had clawed fingers in the middle of their wings, and so their scientific name comes from the ancient Greek *pter*, which means wing, and *dactyl*, which means finger. A second question: Do you know what the Mesozoic era was? Well, *meso* means middle, and *zo* means animal. The Mesozoic era was a geologic era in the earth's history that occurred after the Paleozoic era and before the Cenozoic era, from 230,000,000 years ago until 65,000,000 years ago. The Mesozoic era featured the rise and fall of the dinosaurs and the appearance of birds, grasses, and flowering plants. If you are really adventurous, you will go look up the Paleozoic era, and see what happened then!

Now, let's make some new sentences! I will give you a subject or predicate to start with, and then you can think of your own way to finish the sentence. Sometimes I will give you a subject and leave the predicate blank, and sometimes I will give you a predicate and leave the subject blank. Fill in the blanks with subjects or predicates that help the sentence make sense. For example, if I give you a subject, such as "The star cruiser," you could fill in the predicate blank with a predicate that you imagine. You might complete the sentence by writing, "rumbled toward the icy planet." (Of course, nothing *rumbles* in space, since sound does not carry in a vacuum.)

New Sentences

COMPLETE SUBJECT (What the idea is about)	**COMPLETE PREDICATE** (What we are saying about the subject)
1. F. L. Wright, the famous architect,	_____
2. Egyptian hieroglyphics	_____
3. The red laser beam	_____
4. _____	shone across the Mediterranean.
5. _____	quietly munched the bamboo shoots.
6. _____	climbed aboard the *Hispaniola*.
7. The people of ancient Carthage	_____
8. Beethoven's best symphony	_____
9. _____	is my favorite work of art.
10. _____	littered the laboratory.

Notice that until you completed the subject or predicate, none of your sentences made sense. A subject or a predicate by itself is not an idea; it is only a **fragment**, or piece of an idea. A **sentence fragment** is a piece of a sentence that only makes an incomplete thought. A sentence fragment needs to be finished, just like the subjects and predicates above needed to be finished.

How would I have finished the ten sentences you just worked on? Well, I might have finished them this way:

COMPLETE SUBJECT
(What the idea is about)

COMPLETE PREDICATE
(What we are saying about the subject)

1. **F. L. Wright, the famous architect,** *designed houses to match the landscape.*

2. **Egyptian hieroglyphics** *are made of little pictures.*

3. **The red laser beam** *could be seen from the moon.*

4. *The ship's festive lights* **shone across the Mediterranean.**

5. *The panda bear* **quietly munched the bamboo shoots.**

6. *The wide-eyed, young boy* **climbed aboard the *Hispaniola*.**

7. **The people of ancient Carthage** *waved good-bye to Hannibal.*

8. **Beethoven's best symphony** *is a musical masterpiece.*

9. *Van Gogh's self-portrait* **is my favorite work of art.**

10. *Empty pizza boxes* **littered the laboratory.**

By the way, the *Hispaniola* was the sailing ship in Robert Louis Stevenson's wonderful classic, *Treasure Island,* which is about young Jim Hawkins and his adventures with the dastardly pirates led by Long John Silver. If you have not read this masterpiece, you are in for a great time. I know you would enjoy looking up the famous architect, Frank Lloyd Wright (find photographs of his buildings), as well as the ancient general Hannibal, the great composer Ludwig van Beethoven (listen to a recording of his famous Fifth Symphony), and the Dutch painter Vincent Van Gogh (look at a reproduction of his painting *Starry Night)*.

Now you can make up some sentences of your own. Write the subjects in the blanks at the left, and write the predicates in the blanks at the right. Use your creativity and imagination to write some unexpected and interesting sentences.

Sentences

COMPLETE SUBJECT
(What the idea is **about**)

1.

2.

3.

4.

5.

COMPLETE PREDICATE
(What **we are saying** about the subject)

1.

2.

3.

4.

5.

REVIEW: Now let's look again at the new ideas we have learned about language and sentences.

Our way of putting words together to make our ideas is called **language**.

A two-part thought about something is called an **idea**.

What we are talking about and what we are saying about it are the **two parts of an idea**.
A special way of thinking about language is called **grammar**.
In grammar, we call a two-part idea a **sentence**.
The two parts of the sentence are called the **subject** and the **predicate**.
What the sentence is about is called the **subject**.
What we are saying about the subject is called the **predicate**.
A piece of a sentence that is not complete is only a **fragment**.

What is a sentence like? Now you understand that a sentence is made of two parts—a subject the sentence is about and a predicate that says something about the subject. Think of some other things that also have two parts. For example, an egg has both a white and a yolk inside. A basketball goal has a backboard and a rim. A bicycle wheel has a center and a rim. A person has a first name and a last name. Make a list of things that, like sentences, have two parts. After my first examples, fill in your own.

THE THING	PART ONE	PART TWO
egg	white	yolk
mouth	upper lip	lower lip
shooting an arrow	pull back	let go
echo	sound goes away	sound comes back
_____	_____	_____
_____	_____	_____
_____	_____	_____
_____	_____	_____
_____	_____	_____
_____	_____	_____

Now that you have a list of things that have two parts, which one of these things in your list do you think is really most like a sentence, with its two subject/predicate parts? What is the best comparison? Think about it carefully, and then explain your choice:

Did you enjoy thinking that way? Thinking up comparisons between two different things is a special and important kind of thinking, called *synthesis*. Synthesis is the ability to see connections, or similarities, or relationships between things that seem unconnected at first. When we use synthesis to see hidden connections, we are often surprised to learn how similar things are, and how much everything is connected.

A Vocabulary Note: The word **subject** contains two ancient Latin word pieces, or stems, that we see in many words, **sub** and **ject**. The stem **sub** means "under," and we see **sub** in words such as **submarine** and **submerge**. The stem **ject** means "throw," and we see **ject** in words such as **eject** and **dejected**. So the word **subject** actually contains a picture: the **subject** of a sentence is the part that is "thrown down" for discussion. Look up some of the following example words in your dictionary, and see if you can understand why they mean what they mean:

STEM	MEANING	EXAMPLE WORDS
sub	under	submarine, submerge, subdue, subtract, subside, subordinate
ject	throw	reject, dejected, interject, eject, conjecture, project, adjective, object

▼ 3. Clauses: The Sentences within Sentences

There is another surprising fact about the way we make our ideas into sentences. Many of the sentences that we use are just like the ones we studied above. They have a subject, and then a predicate, and then the sentence ends. Sometimes, however, our ideas get so connected that we like to join simple ideas together into a longer, more complicated idea. In other words, sometimes, we join little related sentences together into a big sentence. For example, we might have these two sentences:

Congress passed the bill. The president signed it into law.

Each of these sentences has its own subject and predicate. But since these two sentences describe something that happened in a connected event, we can connect the sentences together into a longer sentence:

Congress passed the bill, and the president signed it into law.

Now the two little sentences make one long sentence, and it has one subject and predicate, followed by a second subject and predicate, all in one sentence!

<u>Congress</u>   <u>passed the bill,</u>   and   <u>the president</u>   <u>signed it into law.</u>
  subject   predicate   subject   predicate

When we join little sentences this way into a longer sentence of subject/predicate chains, we call each little subject/predicate group a clause.

<u>Congress passed the bill,</u>   and   <u>the president signed it into law.</u>
   first clause   second clause

When there is only one subject/predicate set in the sentence, we say that the sentence has one **clause**.

Our word *clause* comes from the ancient Latin word *claudere* which meant "to close" to the Romans. This makes sense even now because a clause is a group of words in which an idea gets opened, and closed! The idea is opened when we introduce a subject, and then it is closed when we provide the predicate. In a long sentence made of many clauses, we open and close a number of related ideas in a row. Let's look at some examples of clauses in sentences. Notice that each clause has its own subject and its own predicate:

Clauses in Sentences

1. <u>Our forefathers</u>   <u>brought forth upon this continent a new nation.</u>
    subject   predicate

---

a one-clause sentence .

2. I   will arise,   and   I   will go now.
   subj. predicate   subj. predicate

   _____   _____
       first clause   second clause

   _____
                  a two-clause sentence

3. Robert Frost   has miles to go   before   he   sleeps.
     subject   predicate   subj. predicate

   _____   _____
          first clause   second clause

   _____
                  a two-clause sentence

4. When the attack finally begins, you sneak up quietly, and the gang throws balloons.
        subject   predicate   subj.   predicate   subject   predicate

   _____ _____ _____
          first clause   second clause   third clause

   _____
                  a three-clause sentence

   See? We can make long sentences out of any number of related ideas!

   But why is it important to know this?

   By using grammar to inspect our own ideas, we have discovered that our wonderful brains can understand ideas and the relationships between different ideas so well and so quickly that we can connect these ideas into sentences of clauses faster than we can even speak. We can do it without even knowing we are doing it, and before we even have a name for it. It is only now, when we use grammar to inspect our ideas, that we begin to realize what powerful things our minds are. The grammar of clauses shows us how our minds build beautiful structures of ideas.

▼ 4. Parts of Speech: The Kinds of Words

One thing you have noticed about all ideas or sentences: every sentence is made of **words**. A word is a group of sounds or letters that means something. In the sentence, "The famous author Robert Louis Stevenson (1850–1894) wrote the novel, *Treasure Island,*" there are eleven words. For example, *Robert* is a word and *the* is a word. We always put blank spaces between words in a written sentence. If you look at a college dictionary, you will see that we have many thousands of words in our language. In fact, there are far more words than anyone could ever learn!

Just imagine that you traveled to a land far, far away.

(One faraway land is Nepal, near Tibet in the continent of Asia, where Mount Everest, the highest mountain in the world, is. Mount Everest is 29,028 feet high, and it is in the Himalayan mountain range. It is so high that it has only been climbed a few times. Nepal's high-altitude capital is Katmandu. There is a wonderful novel you will want to read one day, *Lost Horizon,* written by James Hilton in 1933, that depicts Nepal under the fictitious name of "Shangri-La.")

Now, just imagine that you travel to a land far, far away, and the gray-bearded king of the land says, "You may have all of the treasures in my kingdom if you can tell me how many kinds of words there are." The king then looks down to the green valleys far, far below, and an icy wind comes down from the frozen peaks above, and blows through your hair.

What would you say? There are thousands and thousands of words in the dictionary. Are there thousands of kinds of words? Are there hundreds of kinds of words?

Well, you are in luck, because if you set off on an adventure one day, you will be prepared with the knowledge that there are only eight kinds of words! Just imagine! All of those words in the dictionary can be put into only eight piles, and the eight different kinds of words are easy to learn. We call the eight kinds of words the eight **parts of speech** because all of our speech can be *parted* into only eight piles of words.

The names of the eight parts of speech are the *noun, pronoun, adjective, verb, adverb, preposition, conjunction,* and *interjection.* In a sentence, each part of speech has something different to do. And since a sentence might only have two words in it, you can tell that not every sentence uses all eight parts of speech. The only parts of speech that have to be in a sentence are the noun or pronoun and the verb. Can you guess why? Let's learn about the eight parts of speech and their functions (uses). As you read the following pages, study the definitions, examples, and discussions of the eight parts of speech carefully and slowly.

The Parts of Speech

PART OF SPEECH	FUNCTION	EXAMPLES
noun (n.)	name of something	*Mary, dog, garden, sound*

A noun is the name of a person, *Picasso,* or the name of a place, *Amsterdam,* or the name of a thing, *aurora.* The sentence *The wind in the willows whispered in the leaves* has three nouns: wind, willows, and leaves. Nouns give us names for things!

Proper nouns are the names of specific people, places, or things. Otherwise, they are common nouns. Study the following examples to see the difference.

Proper Nouns	*Common Nouns*
John	boy
Chicago	city
Statue of Liberty	monument

Nouns can be **singular**, like *dog*, or **plural**, like *dogs*. Proper nouns, like *Istanbul*, are capitalized, but common nouns, like *boy*, are not capitalized.

pronoun (pron.)   **replaces a noun**   *I, she, him, it, them*

A pronoun is a short word that replaces a usually longer noun so that we can speak faster. For example, instead of always saying a person's name, such as *Abraham Lincoln*, in a sentence, we can say *he*. In the sentence *"He was born in a log cabin in Illinois,"* the words *Abraham Lincoln* have been replaced by the short pronoun *he*. Pronouns make language fast!

Two common kinds of pronouns are the **subject pronouns**:

   I, you, he, she, it, we, you, they

and the **object pronouns**:

   me, you, him, her, it, us, you, them.

We have learned that every sentence has a subject and a predicate. Also, every subject contains either a noun or a pronoun. This noun or pronoun that the sentence is about is sometimes called the **simple subject**. The **complete subject** is the simple subject and all the words around it that modify it. Consider the following example:

   The big, brown bear lumbered into the woods.

The word *bear* is the simple subject. *The big, brown bear* is the complete subject.

adjective (adj.)   **modifies a noun or pronoun**   *red, tall, fast, good, the*

To modify is to *change*. An adjective is a word that changes the meaning of a noun or pronoun. For example, for the noun *tree*, we can change it by saying *tall* tree, or *Christmas* tree, or *cherry* tree, and each of these different adjectives changes (we sometimes say *modifies*) the noun and gives us a different picture in our minds. Another example: the noun *garden* could be modified by either the adjective *flower* or the adjective *secret*. We could talk about a *flower* garden, but we could use a different adjective and talk about a *secret* garden instead, and that would modify the idea.

Some adjectives are the opposites of one another: a *fast* car is the opposite of a *slow* car.

The most common adjectives are the three little words *a, an,* and *the.* These three adjectives are called the articles. The word *the* is called the **definite article**, and the words *a* and *an* are called the **indefinite articles**.

Notice that the noun, pronoun, and adjective go together and work together. The nouns name things, the pronouns replace the nouns, and the adjectives modify either nouns or pronouns. You could say that the noun, with its supporting pronouns and adjectives, forms a little noun system, like the sun with its planets.

verb (v.)   **an action or equals word**   *jumps, fell, is*

Every sentence contains a verb, which is sometimes called the **simple predicate**. The **complete predicate** is the simple predicate and all the words around it that modify it. For example:

The big, brown bear lumbered into the woods.

The word *lumbered* is the simple predicate. *Lumbered into the woods* is the complete predicate.

There are two kinds of verbs.

Action verbs show action: they show people and things doing things. Look at the action verbs in these sentences: the dog *barked*. The tall man *grinned*. My best friend *reads* lots of books. We *drove* to Florida. Mary *opened* her brown eyes.

Linking verbs are equals words. They show that two things are the same. For example, in the sentence "Siegfried is a good student." the verb *is* means that Siegfried and the good student are the same person. Siegfried IS the good student.

Action: Michelangelo ran after the ball.
Linking: Michelangelo is good at soccer.

Action: Donatello drew a sketch.
Linking: Donatello is a genius.

Action: Raphael plays baseball in the spring.
Linking: Raphael is a pitcher on the baseball team.

My favorite linking verb sentence is by the poet Marianne Moore, who said that poems *are* imaginary gardens with real toads in them. Don't you like that idea?

G-14

Parts of the Sentence: We have learned about two parts of the sentence already, the **simple subject** and the **simple predicate** or verb. Well, there are two other parts of the sentence you can identify if you know what kind of verb you have. When an action verb sentence shows the subject doing something to something, as in the sentence "The dog bit the mailman," we call the noun or pronoun that receives the action a direct object. When a linking verb sentence shows that the subject is **equal to** something else, as in the sentence "The dog is a poodle," we call the noun or pronoun that is linked to the subject a **subject complement**.

> Direct Object: Achilles grabbed the **warrior**.
> Subject Complement: Achilles was a **warrior**.

Notice that the only way to tell whether the second noun in these sentences is a direct object or a subject complement is to look at the verb. If a sentence contains an action verb, it might have a direct object, but if the sentence contains a linking verb, it might have a subject complement. This is a very advanced grammar idea, and it gives us deep insight into the way we form our own ideas.

Tense: Another very important fact: verbs change, according to the *time* they are describing. The time of the verb is called the verb **tense**. The three most familiar verb tenses are the **present tense**, the **past tense**, and the **future tense**. The verb to *believe*, for example, takes these forms:

> Present tense: I believe in miracles.
> Past tense: I believed in miracles.
> Future tense: I will believe in miracles.

| adverb (adv.) | **modifies a verb, adj., or adv.** | *quickly, slowly, well* |

An adverb is a word that modifies or changes the meaning of a verb, an adjective, or another adverb.

> Adverb modifies verb: I swam *quickly*.
> Adverb modifies adverb: I swam *very* quickly.
> Adverb modifies adjective: I saw a *very* red star.

Before you continue reading, study these three examples very carefully, and make sure you understand every part of speech in every sentence.

Notice that many adverbs end *ly*, such as *quickly, slowly, loudly, nearly, badly,* and *hungrily*.

Notice that the verb and adverb form a little system together. Just as the noun is often accompanied by an adjective, the verb is often accompanied by an adverb that gives it new meaning.

Just as adjectives help us adjust the meanings of nouns when the nouns are not quite what we mean, adverbs help us adjust the meanings of verbs. Adjectives and adverbs are modifiers that help us adjust the meanings of nouns and verbs.

preposition (prep.)   **shows relationship**   *in, on, beside, after*

A preposition is a word that shows how two things are **related** to each other in space or time. Space examples: The dog was *on* the dock. The book is *in* the drawer. The boy was *inside* the secret garden. The garden was *behind* the wall. Time examples: The movie is *after* the news. My birthday is *before* yours. She got sick *during* the game. Prepositions are little words, but they are very important because they show where everything is in space and time. Prepositions let us make ideas that show how the world is arranged!

Another interesting fact about prepositions is that they are always found in little word groups, such as **in** the box, **on** the dock, **under** the bed, **around** the world, and **over** the rainbow. These little word groups always begin with prepositions, and they are called **prepositional phrases**.

In fact, the word *preposition* is made of the Latin *pre*, which means *before*, and the word *position*. A preposition is called a preposition because its **position is always before** the other words in the prepositional phrase! It has the pre-position.

conjunction (conj.)   **joins words**   *and, or, but, so, yet*

A conjunction is a word that joins two other words together into a pair. Michael *and* David ate many hot dogs. By using the conjunction *and*, we can join the two nouns *Michael* and *David* together so we can talk about them both at once, as a pair. We can use a conjunction to join two pronouns: Give the lithograph to him *or* her. If we want to, we can even use a conjunction to join two verbs: Mary thought *and* wondered. We can use a conjunction to join two adverbs: He spoke quickly, *but* confidently. Or we can use a conjunction to join two adjectives: The wall was high *and* dark. Conjunctions let us join things into pairs!

Would you like one more very interesting example? You can even use a conjunction to join two groups of words together. For example, you can use a conjunction to join two prepositional phrases together: The albatross flew over the ship *and* around the mast.

| **interjection (interj.)** | shows emotion | *Oh, wow, yes, no, well* |

Interjections do not do anything special, such as join words, or modify words, or replace words. All they do is show emotion. If we say, "Wow, you look nice!" the word *wow* just shows happiness or excitement. The most common interjections are the words *yes* and *no*. Another very common interjection is the word *oh*: Oh, yes, I like interjections. Do you?

A Vocabulary Note: The word preposition contains two ancient Latin word pieces, or stems, **pre**, and **pos**. We see these stems in many words. The stem **pre** means "before," and we see **pre** in words such as **predict** and **prepare**. The stem **pos** means "put," and we see **pos** in words such as **position** and **depose**. So the word preposition contains a picture: the **preposition** is the part that is "put before" the other words in the phrase. The word **conjunction** also contains stems which appear in many other words: **con** and **junct**. The stem **con** means "together," and the stem **junct** means "join." In the words **adverb** and **adjective**, we see the stem **ad**, which means "to," and the word **pronoun** contains the stem **pro**, which means "for" or sometimes "forward." Look up some of the following example words in your dictionary, and see if you can understand why they mean what they mean:

STEM	MEANING	EXAMPLE WORDS
pre	before	predict, prepare, preliminary, preschool, preface, premonition
pos	put	position, depose, interpose, suppose, deposit, repose
con	together	conjunction, contact, connect, contiguous, contract, converge
junct	join	juncture, disjunction, injunction, adjunct, conjunction
ad	to	adjective, adverb, adherent, adjacent, adapt, admit
pro	for/forward	pronoun, propel, prophet, proponent, prominent, promote

Now, you know that the stem **ject** means "throw." In the word **object**, however, we also see the stem **ob**. which means "toward" or "about." We see the stem **ob** in many words: *object, obstacle, obdurate, oblique, obloquy, objurgate,* and *obscure,* for example. Use your dictionary to look up the full etymology of the word *object* and see if you can understand why we call objects *objects*. Then answer this question: *How are direct objects in sentences similar to objects on the ground?*

REVIEW: Let's look again at what the eight kinds of words do. Study the parts of speech until you have their functions memorized. Make sure that you can remember some examples of each one.

| **noun** | name of something | Mike, dog, tree, sound |

The *boy* listened to the *music* of Verdi.

| **pronoun** | replaces a noun | I, she, him, it, them |

She and *I* saw *him* and *her* at the Museum of Modern Art.

| **adjective** | modifies a noun or pronoun | red, tall, fast, good, the |

Isaac Newton, *a famous* mathematician, discovered *the natural* law.

| **verb** | an action or equals word | jumps, fell, is |

I *lost* the Byron poem yesterday, but I *have* it now.

| **adverb** | modifies a verb | quickly, slowly, well |

The pianist played her Chopin solo *beautifully*.

| **preposition** | shows relationship | in, on, beside, after |

The government is *of* the people, *by* the people, and *for* the people.

| **conjunction** | joins words | and, or, but |

I saw the doctor, *and* she gave me some medicine.

| **interjection** | shows emotion | Oh, wow, yes, no, well |

Oh, yes, I always vote in the elections.

Examples. Now let's look at some sentences, and inspect the parts of speech in each one. We will use a little arrow, like this →, to show what noun an adjective modifies, or to show what verb an adverb modifies.

```
    adj. →    n.           v.       adj.→   n.
1. The    architect    designed    a    bridge.
        subject                 predicate
```

Notice that the noun *bridge* is a direct object of the action verb *designed*.

```
       n.          adv.→      v.      adj. →    n.
2. Michelangelo   carefully   painted   the   ceiling.
       subject                  predicate
```

Notice that the noun *ceiling* is a direct object of the action verb *painted*.

```
  interj.  pron.  conj. pron.  v.       n.
3. Yes,    you   and   I     are   friends.
              subject       predicate
```

Notice that the noun *friends* is a subject complement of the linking verb *are*.

G-18

```
         n.        v.      prep.     adj.→    n.
4. Magellan     sailed    around    the     planet.
     subject                        predicate
```

```
        n.       conj.    pron.    n.     prep.        n.           v.
5. Alexander    and      his     army    of    Macedonians     won.
                          subject                              predicate
```

Now, notice some very interesting things about the grammar of these sentences:

▼ The subject can be one word or many words.

▼ The predicate can be one word or many words.

▼ The main word of the subject is always a noun or pronoun.

▼ The main word of the predicate is always a verb.

▼ A sentence always contains a noun or pronoun and a verb.

You try it. Here are some more sentences. Study each one carefully and imitate the five examples above by writing the abbreviation for the part of speech above each word, and by underlining the subject and predicate of each sentence. Identify any direct objects or subject complements you see.

1. **The   scientist   used   a   microscope.**

2. **Rembrandt   slowly   painted   the   canvas.**

3. **Yes,   he   and   she   were   members.**

4. **De Soto   floated   down   the   Mississippi.**

5. **Spartacus   and   his   force   of   gladiators   lost.**

Check your answers from the answer key on the next page.

Answer Key

$$\text{adj.} \rightarrow \quad \text{n.} \qquad \text{v.} \qquad \text{adj.} \rightarrow \quad \text{n.}$$

1. **The   scientist   used   a   microscope.**

       subject   predicate

The noun *microscope* is a direct object.

$$\qquad\quad \text{n.} \qquad \text{adj.} \rightarrow \quad \text{v.} \qquad \text{adj.} \rightarrow \quad \text{n.}$$

2. **Rembrandt   slowly   painted   the   canvas.**

   subject   predicate

The noun *canvas* is a direct object.

$$\text{interj.} \quad \text{pron.} \quad \text{conj.} \quad \text{pron.} \qquad \text{v.} \qquad \text{n.}$$

3. **Yes,   he   and   she   were   members.**

           subject   predicate

The noun *members* is a subject complement.

$$\quad\; \text{n.} \qquad \text{v.} \qquad \text{prep.} \quad \text{adj.} \rightarrow \quad \text{n.}$$

4. **De Soto   floated   down   the   Mississippi.**

  subject   predicate

$$\quad\;\; \text{n.} \qquad \text{conj.} \quad \text{pron.} \quad \text{n.} \quad \text{prep.} \qquad \text{n.} \qquad \text{v.}$$

5. **Spartacus   and   his   force   of   gladiators   lost.**

               subject   predicate

(I know, you want to know who Rembrandt, De Soto, and Spartacus were. Well, Rembrandt van Rijn was a Dutch master painter who was born in 1606 and died in 1669. Rembrandt did a self-portrait that is one of the most striking and penetrating in the history of art. Hernando De Soto was a courageous Spanish explorer, born about 1500, who is credited with discovering the Mississippi River, although the American Indians had actually discovered it long, long before any Europeans arrived in the New World. Spartacus was a proud Thracian slave in the Roman Empire who became a gladiator and who led a slave revolt against Rome. Spartacus and his men were annihilated in 71 B.C.)

Now, think about this: One day, long, long ago, some human being uttered the first word, and language began. Over a period of time, human beings developed language, and more and more parts of speech were created, until there were eight. Use your common sense and imagination to guess what you think was probably the part of speech of the first words ever used. Think about it, and then write down your guess, and the reason you think it is probable.

The part of speech of the first word was _____ .

I think this because:

▼ 5. Phrases: The Clever Teamwork

We all know what teams are. Five players work together on a basketball team, and each player has his or her own part in executing a well-practiced play. Cheerleaders work together to make a single pyramid, with each cheerleader standing on the shoulders of two cheerleaders below. Lawyers can work as a team to win a single case. Computer programmers work in teams to write programs; each programmer specializes in writing a different part of the computer code.

Well, by inspecting our own ideas with grammar, we have discovered a remarkable thing. Sometimes, a whole group of words will team together to imitate a single part of speech! A team of words acting as a single part of speech is called a **phrase**. We learned a bit about **prepositional phrases** when we studied the parts of speech, but now we are ready to learn more. Here is a more complete definition of the phrase: *a phrase is a group of words that acts as a single part of speech, and that does not contain a subject and its predicate.* For example, notice that a prepositional phrase can behave as though it were an adverb, modifying a verb:

An ordinary adverb: The penguin sat **there**.
A phrase: The penguin sat **on the iceberg**.

In each case, the verb *sat* is being modified by something, but in the first example the verb is being modified by a simple adverb, *there*, whereas in the second example, the verb is being modified by a group of words, *on the iceberg*, acting as a team to make an adverb. That is what phrases are: word groups imitating other parts of speech. It is interesting, by the way, to note that our English word *phrase* comes from a very ancient Greek word, *phrazein*, which meant "to speak."

A prepositional phrase can also act as an adjective:

An ordinary adjective: The **top** book is a classic.
A phrase: The book **on the top** is a classic.

There are different kinds of phrases. Let's look at some other phrases, and see some of the interesting forms that phrases can take in sentences. Remember to notice that the phrase never contains both a sentence's subject and its predicate, and that a sentence can contain more than one phrase, or no phrase at all.

Phrases

Carmen, **my favorite opera**, is by the composer Bizet.
Not remembering names is my problem.
Birds fly **over the rainbow**.
I pledge allegiance **to the flag**.
The assault team climbed the north face of **Mount Everest**.
Magellan sailed **around the world**.
Newton loved **to study mathematics**.
The painting **on the museum's north wall** was painted **by the French painter Monet**.

▼ Conclusion

Now, let's think carefully about all of the things that we have learned. We have learned a very important secret about the way we think and express our ideas about the world. The secret is that our ideas, which we sometimes call sentences, are only complete when they are made of two parts. These two parts are the subject that the sentence is about, and the predicate that says something about the subject. If we do not have both of these parts in our ideas, we will not have a complete thought, and we will not make any sense to anyone else. Other people have to know both of these parts in order to understand our ideas; they have to know what we are talking about, and they have to know what we are saying about it.

We also learned that sometimes simple sentences can be connected together into more complicated ideas, and then we say that each little subject/predicate group inside the long sentence is a clause.

We have also learned an amazing secret about the thousands and thousands of words in our English language: there are only eight kinds! We call these eight kinds of words the **parts of speech**. We have learned that each kind of word has a special purpose, a function, in a sentence. Two of the parts of speech, the **noun** and the **verb**, are special, because they are in almost every sentence. The **subject** of a sentence usually has a noun (but it might have a **pronoun** instead to take the noun's place), and the predicate of the sentence always (yes, always) has a verb.

In studying the parts of speech, we learned that they are used as **parts of the sentence**. The **simple subject** is the noun or pronoun that the sentence is about. The **simple predicate** is the subject's verb. The **direct object** is a noun or pronoun that receives the action of the action verb, and the **subject complement** is the noun or pronoun linked to the subject by the linking verb.

We have learned that our minds are clever enough to collect little groups of words together into **phrases** that imitate other parts of speech, and we have seen examples of phrases acting as adverbs, as adjectives, and even as nouns (if you did not notice that, go back and look closely at the examples of phrases).

Finally, **verbs** have taught us a very important secret about ideas. Since there are two kinds of verbs, the **action** kind and the **equals or linking** kind, this means that there are two main kinds of ideas. We can either say that the **subject is doing something**, or we can say that the **subject is something**. For example, we can use an action verb and say, "The reader of this book *saw* a very good student." But if we use a linking/equals verb, we can say something even better: "The reader of this book *is* a very good student."

                adj.   n.   prep. adj.   n.   v. adj. adv. adj.   n.
The   reader   of this book   is   a   very   good   student.
                        prep. phrase
     simple subj.   simple pred.   subject complement

_____   _____
     complete subject   complete predicate

_____
                         a one-clause sentence

See if you can analyze the following sentence as I analyzed the one above:

We   inspect   ideas   with   grammar.

Check the next page for an analysis of this sentence.

pronoun	verb	noun	preposition	noun
We	**inspect**	**ideas**	**with**	**grammar.**
simple subject	simple predicate	direct object		

subject	complete predicate

a one-clause sentence

The last word: As you see, grammar is a fascinating way to think about our own thinking. By using grammar, we can examine our thoughts, and we can see how we have made those thoughts. If we did not have grammar, we would never really be able to understand how powerful our minds are. After this short introduction to grammar, however, you have begun to understand how powerfully your mind makes ideas out of language. As you learn more and more about grammar in the future, you will gain greater insight into how wonderful it is to be a human being, an idea-maker. I hope that you will always look forward to the wonderful study of grammar. It is truly a way of inspecting our own ideas.

SECTION

IV

IMPLEMENTATION

This section includes guidelines for unit implementation in classrooms and outlines the instructional models employed in the unit.

▼ Classroom Guidelines for Unit Implementation

The following pages outline some guidelines for teachers on implementing the unit effectively in classrooms. Comments from teachers who piloted the unit have been used in developing these recommendations.

Target Population

This unit was designed for use with high-ability fifth through seventh grade students. It has been piloted with such students in various settings and found effective with respect to learning gains. In heterogeneous settings, the unit has been used with a broader range of students and found effective as well, provided that teachers have modified the reading selections.

Use of the Unit in Relation to Existing Language Arts Curriculum

This unit is intended to represent a semester's work in language arts for high-ability learners. Thus, whoever teaches the unit should assign the grade for language arts and note individual progress based on the goals of the unit. (See **Overall Student Assessment Report** at the end of Lesson 24.) Because the unit does not include specific lesson emphases on spelling, developmental reading skills, or narrative writing, it is recommended that these elements be considered for use during a second semester of language arts. Supplemental materials might include *Junior Great Books, Write Source 2000, The Magic Lens*, and *Word within the Word.* (See Bibliography of Teacher Resources in Section V for references.)

Alignment of the Unit with National Standards

This unit of study has been aligned with the English standards developed by the National Council of Teachers of English (NCTE) and the International Reading Association (IRA). It responds well to all major aspects of those standards, while incorporating a rigorous assessment component to enhance individual student progress during and at the conclusion of the unit. The alignment process has also been done for individual state documents in language arts, including those of Connecticut, New York, South Carolina, Texas, and Virginia. Selected district alignments have also been completed.

The chart on the following page represents the NCTE/IRA alignment:

Alignment with NCTE/IRA Standards

Standards for the English Language Arts	William and Mary Language Arts Units
1. Students read a wide range of print and nonprint texts to build an understanding of texts, of themselves, and of the cultures of the United States and the world; to acquire new information; to respond to the needs and demands of society and the workplace; and for personal fulfillment.	Emphasis on multicultural and global literature and broad-based reading.
2. Students read a wide range of literature from many periods in many genres to build an understanding of the many dimensions (e.g., philosophical, ethical, aesthetic) of human experience.	Broad-based reading in poetry, short story, biography, essay, and novel forms.
3. Students apply a wide range of strategies to comprehend, interpret, evaluate, and appreciate texts.	Major goal on analysis and interpretation of literature. (Goal 1)
4. Students adjust their use of spoken, written, and visual language to communicate effectively with a variety of audiences and for different purposes.	Sensitivity to audience built into writing and research activities.
5. Students employ a wide range of strategies as they write and use different writing process elements appropriately.	Major outcome related to effective use of all stages of the writing process. (Goal 2)
6. Students apply knowledge of language structure, language conventions, media techniques, figurative language, and genre to create, critique, and discuss print and nonprint texts.	Major goal of developing linguistic competency. (Goal 3)
7. Students conduct research on issues and interests by generating ideas and questions and by posing problems. They gather, evaluate, and synthesize data from a variety of sources to communicate their discoveries in ways that suit their purpose and audience.	Research project that focuses on these skills based on issue identification is a feature of each unit; the use of the reasoning model underlies the teaching of all language arts strands. (Goal 5)
8. Students use a wide variety of technological and informational resources to gather and synthesize information and to create and communicate knowledge.	Incorporated in research model and writing task demands.
9. Students develop an understanding of and respect for diversity in language use, patterns, and dialects across cultures, ethnic groups, geographic regions, and social roles.	Applicable to the context of selected literature.
10. Students whose first language is not English make use of their first language to develop competency in the English language arts and understanding of content across the curriculum.	N/A
11. Students participate as knowledgeable, reflective, creative, and critical members of a variety of literacy communities.	Contact with authors, use of peer review, major discussions of literary works.
12. Students use spoken, written, and visual language to accomplish their own purposes.	Integrated throughout the units.

Schedule for Unit Implementation

For purposes of this unit, a lesson is defined as at least one two-hour session. It is preferable that the unit be taught across a two-hour block that encompasses both reading and language arts time allocations. A minimum of fifty total instructional hours should be allocated for teaching this unit. Teachers are encouraged to expand this schedule based on available time and student interest. Many teachers have used the unit for a full semester of work. Ideally, this curriculum should be taught in a setting in which the class meets on a daily basis.

Grouping

The unit has been implemented in a variety of classroom grouping models, including heterogeneous classrooms, pull-out programs, and self-contained gifted classes. Based on our feedback from national pilots, we suggest that school districts employ their existing grouping approach to teach the unit the first time. Based on individual district results from the first year of implementation, decisions about regrouping procedures may be explored. The comments that follow relate to implementation tips for each setting:

Inclusion or Heterogeneous Classrooms

▼ In this type of setting, it is recommended that teachers differentiate the readings for implementation. Unit readings are clearly intended for advanced readers.

▼ It is also advisable to cluster group students based on reading selections for discussion of these readings.

▼ All students can benefit from learning the fundamental teaching models employed in the unit.

▼ The research project may be modified for students, based on individual level of functioning.

Pull-out Programs

▼ Students must meet at least two hours per week in order to implement this unit.

▼ Consider cross-grade grouping in order to implement this unit.

▼ Continuity of ideas is the challenge in implementing this unit. It is essential that homework be assigned and completed, even within a pull-out program that does not meet daily.

Self-contained Gifted Classes

▼ In this setting, the unit needs to be supplemented with other materials and resources. Use of *Junior Great Books* to enhance literature study is recommended. Michael Thompson's materials in vocabulary and grammar are also recommended. (See Bibliography of Teacher Resources in Section V for references.)

▼ Cluster grouping is encouraged to ensure that advanced readers are grouped together.

Use of Learning Centers

Learning Centers should be set up and made available for student use throughout the course of the unit. They help to provide a change of pace during large time blocks of instruction as well as allowing students to explore topics of interest more fully. They are introduced in the lesson plans as they become relevant to the aspects of the unit being studied. (See below for indication of the lessons in which each Learning Center is introduced.) Learning Centers may be managed as the teacher sees fit, with specific times assigned to these activities or on a less structured basis. It would be helpful to have an assistant to interact with students and answer questions during Learning Center time. Some recording system should be established; a notebook of student records may be kept at each Learning Center, or students may keep records in their individual unit notebooks.

a. **Language Study Center** (Lesson 3)

This Learning Center is intended to provide students with additional opportunities to study language. A set of teacher-made task cards should be kept at the Center with short tasks or projects for students; they may keep a record in their notebooks of task card responses. Task cards may include several activities with different levels of difficulty, and points or scores may be assigned accordingly if the teacher chooses. Several sample task cards are listed below:

Card 1: *Write the sentence below on a card. Ask at least ten people to read it out loud. Note the way they pronounce the word "February." Look up the pronunciation in a good dictionary. Write a paragraph telling about your "pronunciation survey" and its results.*

Valentine's Day comes in February.

Card 2: *Make two word banks that list words that can be used to describe the action of a) eating and b) drinking. Then substitute an appropriate form of each into the following sentence to see how much difference each makes in the meaning.*

Alfred _____ the milk and _____ the cookies.

Card 3: *Look for some words that do not contain the letters **a, e, i, o,** or **u.** List them.*

Card 4: *Look up the word "anagram" in a dictionary.*

  a) *Write the definition.*

  b) *Analyze the meaning of the word using the Latin meanings of the parts of the word.*

  c) *Make a list of 20 pairs of words that are anagram pairs.*

Card 5: *Look up the meanings of the words "further" and "farther." Write an explanation of how each should be used. Then write each one in a sentence.*

b. **Unit Vocabulary Center** (Lesson 3)

At this Learning Center, a list of new vocabulary words encountered in the unit readings should be kept and regularly updated. (See Introduction to Section II for a list of words.)

Dictionaries and blank copies of the Vocabulary Web should be kept at the Center, as well as copies of student readings. Students visiting the Center may work alone or in small groups to develop Vocabulary Webs from unit words, either compiling individual notebooks of webs or a class notebook. This Center allows students to gain more practice with the Vocabulary Web, as class time will not allow all of the new words to be studied in depth.

c. **Writing/Computer Center** (Lesson 5)

At this Learning Center, students have the opportunity to practice the stages of writing and the format of the persuasive paragraph. Writing materials and a word processing program should be made available to students, along with a list of suggested writing topics. Students may compose paragraphs and longer pieces at the Writing/Computer Center, may work in pairs to critique one another's work, and may revise, edit, and publish their work. This Center may be used to work on unit assignments and/or on separate extension activities.

d. **Persuasive Speaking Center** (Lesson 6)

At this Learning Center, have available videos of speeches which students may watch and analyze according to their growing understanding of elements of persuasion. Encourage them to evaluate the speeches they watch, using the materials they are given to evaluate presentations in class. The Center should also have available a list of prompts for persuasive speeches students may develop and deliver themselves to a small group of peers or to the class.

e. **Research Center** (Lesson 11)

This Learning Center may include a regular and an electronic encyclopedia, nonfiction books, and other resources which will help students in investigating their issue. A list of guiding questions and key terms to investigate may help students in their research efforts. In addition, this Center may include nonfiction materials about the authors whose works are included in the unit as well as the people, places, and things described in the readings, so that students may pursue areas of interest.

Use of Technology

Various elements of technology are used to enhance the effectiveness of the unit.

▼ A word processing program may be used for writing, revising, and editing written work. Students should be expected to use a spell checker to assist in the editing process.

▼ The research strand requires students to locate data and evidence to support various points of view on their issue. The following information-gathering tools may be useful to students as they seek ideas and information. Teachers should ensure that students understand each information source and how to access it:

　　▼ CD-ROM library databases

　　▼ Interview or survey by electronic mail

- ▼ Specific resource materials on CD-ROM such as an encyclopedia, atlas, or other reference materials
- ▼ World Wide Web

Collaboration with Librarians

Because literature and information play key roles in the search for meaning, this unit depends on rich and extensive library resources. Working with librarians is essential for both teachers and students throughout the unit. Teachers and school librarians should work together in the planning stages of the unit to tailor the literature and research demands to the interests and abilities of the students. Because many of the resources suggested in this unit exceed the scope of school libraries, public and academic librarians should also be involved in the planning and implementation. Librarians can suggest resources, obtain materials on interlibrary loan, and work with students on research projects.

Students should be encouraged to become acquainted with the librarians in their community for several reasons. First, libraries are complex systems of organizing information. The systems vary from one library to another, and technological access to the systems is constantly changing. Librarians serve as expert guides to the information maze, and they are eager to assist library users. Secondly, the most important skill in using the library is knowing how to ask questions. Students should learn that working with a librarian is not a one-time inquiry or plea for assistance, but an interactive communication and discovery process. As the student asks a question and the librarian makes suggestions, the student will gain a better understanding of the topic and find new questions and ideas to explore. To maximize the use of library resources, the student should then discuss these new questions and ideas with the librarian. Learning to use the services of librarians and other information professionals is an important tool for lifelong learning.

▼ Teaching Models

There are seven teaching models that are used consistently throughout the unit to ensure emphasis on unit outcomes. It is suggested that teachers become familiar with these models and how to implement them before using the unit. The models are listed below and outlined in the pages that follow.

1. The Taba Model of Concept Development
2. Literature Web Model
3. Vocabulary Web Model
4. Hamburger Model for Persuasive Writing
5. The Writing Process Model
6. Elements of Reasoning
7. Research Model

The Taba Model of Concept Development

The concept development model used in the unit, based on Hilda Taba's Concept Development model (Taba, 1962), involves both inductive and deductive reasoning processes. Used as a beginning lesson in the unit (**Lesson 2**), the model focuses on the creation of generalizations from a student-derived list of created concepts. The model is comprised of five steps and involves student participation at every step. Students begin with a broad concept, determine specific examples from that, create appropriate categorization systems, establish a generalization from those categories, and then apply the generalization to their readings and other situations.

This model is best employed by dividing the class into small groups of 4–5 for initial work, followed by whole class discussion after each stage of the process. The explanation below illustrates the use of the model around the concept of change, the central idea of this unit.

1. Students generate examples of the concept of change, derived from their own understanding and experiences with changes in the world. Teachers should encourage students to provide at least 25 examples.

2. Once an adequate number of examples has been elicited, students then group examples together into categories. Such a process allows students to search for interrelatedness and to organize materials. Students should explain their reasoning for given categories and seek clarification from each other as a whole class. Teachers should ensure that students have accounted for all of their examples through the categories established.

3. Students are now asked to think of non-examples of the concept of change. Teachers may begin the brainstorming process with the direction, "Now list examples of things that *do not change*." Teachers should encourage students to think carefully about non-examples and discuss ideas within their groups. Each group should list five to six examples.

4. The students now determine generalizations about the concept of change, using their lists of examples and nonexamples. Generalizations might include such ideas as "Change may be positive or negative" and "Change is linked to time." Generalizations should be derived from student input and may not precisely reflect the unit generalizations. Teachers should post the students' best generalizations on one side of the room and the prescribed unit generalizations on the other. Each set should be referred to throughout the unit.

5. Throughout the unit, students are asked to identify specific examples of the generalizations from their own readings, or to describe how the concept of change applies to a given situation about which they have read. Students are also asked to apply the generalizations to their own writings and their own lives.

Source: Taba, H. (1962). *Curriculum development: Theory and practice.* NY: Harcourt, Brace & World, Inc.

Practice webs using the generalizations about change are structured into core lessons in the unit. A change matrix which asks students to link ideas about change to the literature they read is used throughout the unit. A final assessment on how well students understand the concept of change may also be found in **Lesson 23**.

The concept of change is discussed more fully in a paper to be found in the appendix.

Key lessons focusing on the concept of change are listed below.

▼ **Lesson 2**

▼ **Lesson 4**

▼ **Lesson 7**

▼ **Lesson 9**

▼ **Lesson 10**

▼ **Lesson 12**

▼ **Lesson 14**

▼ **Lesson 15**

▼ **Lesson 17**

▼ **Lesson 20**

▼ **Lesson 23**

▼ **Lesson 24**

Literature Web Model

The Literature Web model encourages students to consider five aspects of a selection they are reading: key words (important, interesting, intriguing, surprising, or unknown to the reader), feelings (those of the reader), images or symbols, ideas, and structure of writing (anything you notice about how the piece is written, such as dialogue, rhyming, short sentences, or big words). The web helps students to organize their initial responses and provides them with a platform for discussing the piece in small or large groups. Whenever possible, students should be allowed to underline and to make marginal notes as they read and reread. After marking the text, they then organize their notes into the web.

The Literature Web is introduced in **Lesson 4**; suggested questions for completing and discussing the web are described below:

a. **Key Words:** Think and look back over the story. What were some words or groups of words that you really liked or thought were really important? Why were they special words to you? What were some words that you thought were interesting or exciting?

b. **Feelings:** What feelings did you get when you read the story? What feelings do you think the characters had? What happened in the story to tell you how the characters were feeling? Why do you think you had the feelings that you did?

c. **Ideas:** What was the main idea of the story? What were some of the other ideas the author was trying to talk about? What was she saying about change?

d. **Images:** What were some of the pictures that came to your mind as you read the story? What were some things about the story that may have had more than one meaning?

e. **Structure of Writing:** What are some important characteristics of the way this piece is put together? How does the rhyming pattern (or dialogue, short sentences, etc.) contribute to the piece? How is the structure important for the meaning of the piece?

After students have completed their webs individually, they should compare their webs in small groups. This initial discussion will enable them to consider the ideas of others and to understand that individuals interpret literature differently. These small groups may compile a composite web that includes the ideas of all members.

Following the small group work, teachers have several options for using the webs. For instance, they may ask each group to report to the class; they may ask groups to post their composite webs; or they may develop a new web with the class based on the small group work. However, each web serves to prepare students to consider various issues the teacher will raise in whole group discussion. It is important that teachers hold a whole group discussion as the final aspect of implementing the model as a teaching-learning device. Teachers are encouraged to post the poem or story under consideration on an overhead or wherever it can be seen as the discussion is held. The teacher should record ideas, underline words listed, and call attention to student responses visually.

The Literature Web is employed in the following lessons:

▼ **Lesson 3**

▼ **Lesson 4**

▼ **Lesson 7**

▼ **Lesson 9**

▼ **Lesson 10**

▼ **Lesson 12**

▼ **Lesson 15**

▼ **Lesson 18**

▼ **Lesson 20**

▼ **Lesson 21**

▼ Literature Web Model

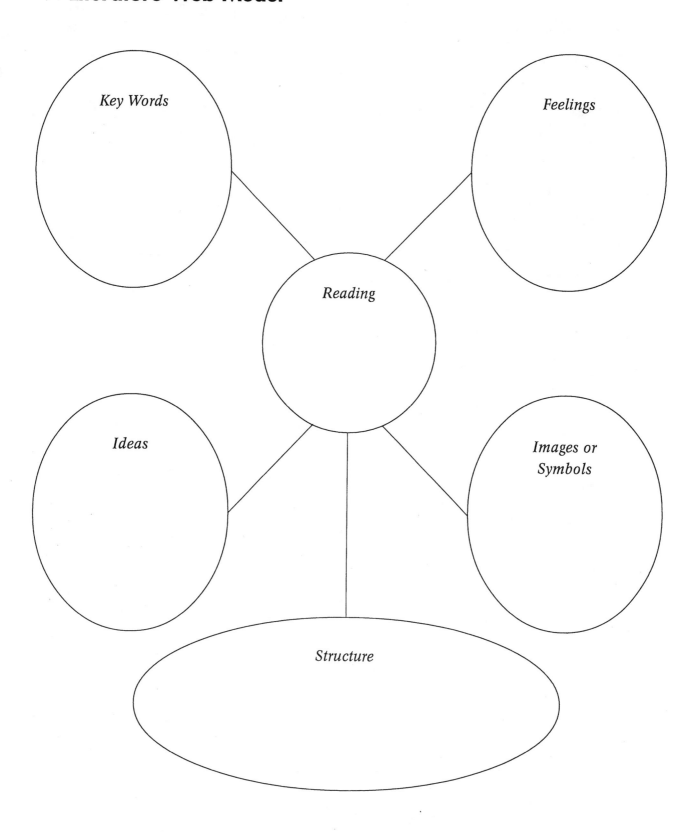

▼ Vocabulary Web Model

The purpose of the Vocabulary Web model is to enable students to gain an in-depth understanding of interesting words. Rather than promoting superficial vocabulary development, the web approach allows for deep student processing of challenging and interesting words.

An example of a vocabulary web activity is given below. The teacher should introduce the activity by exploring the web with the whole class. This is introduced in **Lesson 3**; general steps are listed below, with the word *diverge* as an example:

1. Introduce a **Vocabulary Web**. Put students in groups of no more than four, with a dictionary available as a resource in each group. Distribute copies of a blank Vocabulary Web and ask students to write the word *diverge* in the center. Ask for an explanation of what the word means within the context of a given piece of literature. Have students find the word in the story and write the sentence in which it is found in the "Sentence" cell of the Vocabulary Web.

2. Ask students to look in their dictionaries to find the definition of the word. Display an enlarged copy of the definition on the board or overhead. Have students write the definition relevant to the story into the "Definition" cell of the Vocabulary Web.

3. In their groups, have students develop their own sentences using the word. Ask them to write the sentence in the "Example" cell.

4. Discuss the meanings of the words *synonym* and *antonym*. Have students check the dictionary and think about possible synonyms and antonyms for the word and fill them into the appropriate cells. (Note: Not all cells must be filled for all words; there may not be synonyms and antonyms for all of the words studied.)

5. Ask students what is meant by the phrase "part of speech." Have them locate the part of the dictionary definition that identifies a word's part of speech. Students should then write the part of speech for the word *diverge* into their group webs.

6. Encourage students to think about the *stems* of the word, or the smaller words and pieces of words from which the larger word is made. These include prefixes, suffixes, and roots. Encourage students to check the dictionary for possible stems. Write any identified stems into the appropriate cell of the Vocabulary Web.

7. Have students locate the origin of the word (Latin, French, Greek, etc.) in the definition and write it in the "Origin" cell of the Vocabulary Web.

8. Ask students to think of other words in the same family as the word *diverge*, or other words which use one or more of the same stems. Encourage them to use their ideas from the stems cell to give them ideas.

9. Discuss the Vocabulary Webs developed by the student groups.

Note: Students may also add any number of extensions to the main circles if they identify additional information about the word.

Once students become familiar with this activity, they should use a streamlined version to accommodate new words they meet in their independent reading. A vocabulary section should be kept in a separate place in students' notebooks for this purpose. They need list only the word, definition, and sentence in which the word was encountered, plus any additional information they find particularly interesting, and they may then develop webs for a few selected words. *The American Heritage Dictionary of the English Language* (Third Edition) is recommended for this purpose.

The Vocabulary Web is employed in the following lessons of the unit:

▼ **Lesson 3**

▼ **Lesson 4**

▼ **Lesson 9**

▼ **Lesson 12**

▼ **Lesson 14**

▼ **Lesson 16**

▼ **Lesson 18**

▼ **Lesson 21**

▼ Vocabulary Web Model

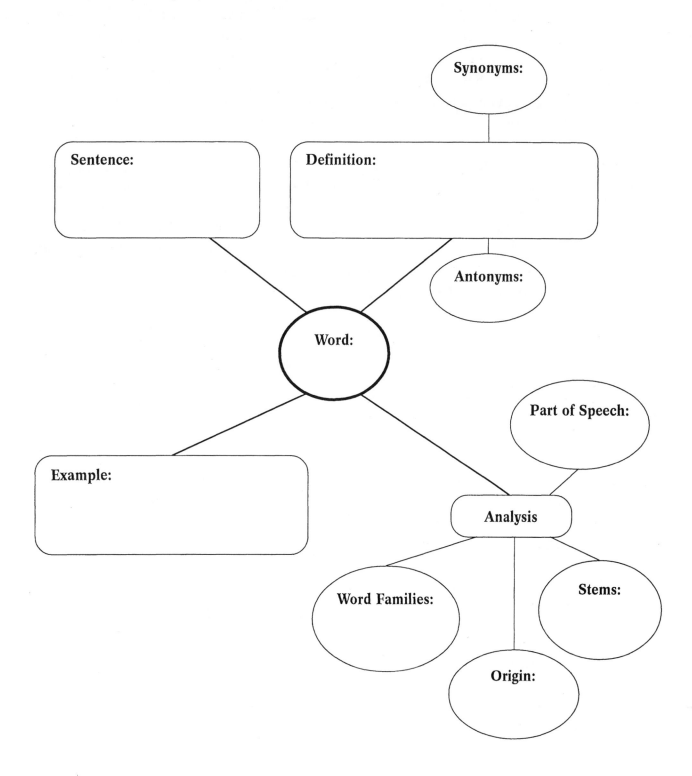

▼ The Hamburger Model for Persuasive Writing

The purpose of the Hamburger Model is to provide students with a useful metaphor to aid them in developing a persuasive paragraph or essay. The model should be introduced by the teacher, showing students that the top bun and the bottom bun represent the introduction and conclusion of any persuasive writing piece. The teacher should note that the reasons given in support of the thesis statement are like the meat or vegetables in a hamburger, providing the major substance of the sandwich. Elaboration represents the condiments in a sandwich, the ketchup, mustard, and onions that hold a sandwich together, just as examples and illustrations hold a persuasive writing piece together.

Teachers now should show students examples of hamburger paragraphs and essays (see **Lesson 5**) and have students find the top bun, bottom bun, hamburger, and condiments. Discuss how "good" each sandwich is.

Teachers may now ask students to construct their own "hamburger" paragraphs. After students have constructed their own paragraphs, teachers may use peer and self assessments to have students judge their own and one another's writing. This process should be repeated throughout the unit.

The Hamburger Model is addressed in the following lessons:

▼ **Lesson 5**

▼ **Lesson 8**

▼ **Lesson 9**

▼ **Lesson 12**

▼ **Lesson 20**

▼ **Lesson 22**

▼ **Lesson 23**

▼ **Lesson 24**

▼ The Hamburger Model for Persuasive Writing

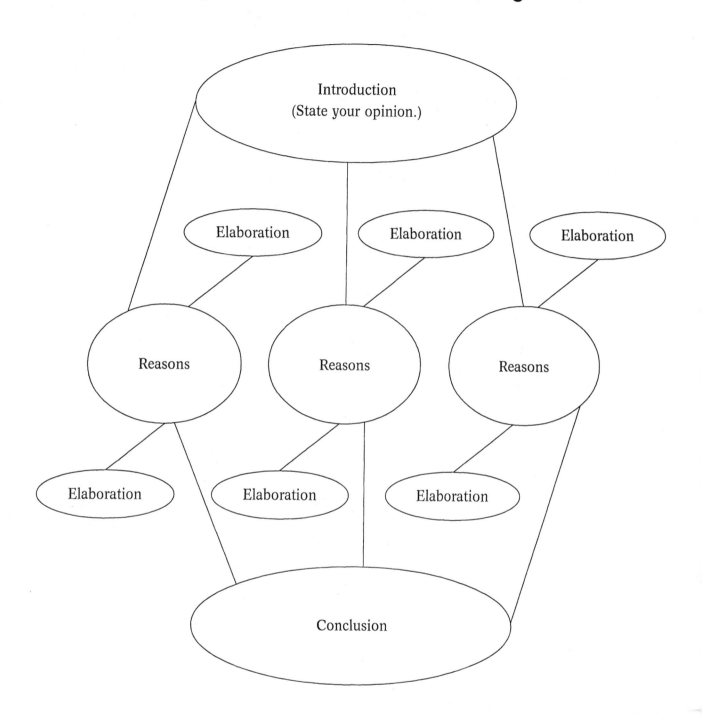

▼ The Writing Process Model

The writing process shows the stages that writers use to develop a written composition. The stages are not separate parts that writers go through from one to five; rather, writers move back and forth among the stages and use them to construct, clarify, and polish their writing. The writing process model is used throughout the unit to encourage students to engage in actively improving their own writing.

1. *Prewriting:* List your ideas and begin to organize them. You may want to use a graphic organizer such as a web or a Venn diagram. Graphic organizers help you to "see" what you will write about. As you write, you can add to your diagram or change it.

2. *Drafting:* Write a rough draft, getting your ideas onto paper and not worrying about mechanics such as spelling, grammar, or punctuation. Some writers call this stage "composing." Sometimes the first draft is a "messing around" stage in which your drafting or composing helps you to "hear" what you want to say.

3. *Revising:* Conferencing is an essential step in the revising stage. Ask people (friends, family, teachers) to read and listen to your work and to tell you what they like, what they don't understand, and what they'd like to know more about. This is the place to make major changes in your "composition" or draft. Sometimes you may want to go back to the prewriting stage and redo your organizer so that your paper has a new structure.

4. *Editing:* After you have revised your paper, look for the small changes that will make a big difference. Check your choice of words and identify mechanical errors. After you make the changes and corrections, proofread your work one final time. You may want to ask a friend or an adult for help.

5. *Sharing or Publishing:* There are numerous ways to share and to publish your work. You can bind it into a book, recopy it in your best handwriting and post it on a bulletin board, read it aloud to your class or family, or make it into a gift for someone special.

▼ Elements of Reasoning

The reasoning strand used throughout the unit focuses on eight elements identified by Richard Paul (1992). It is embedded in all lessons of the unit through questions, writing assignments, and research work. These elements of thought are the basic building blocks of productive thinking. Working together, they provide a general logic to reasoning. In literature interpretation and listening, they help one make sense of the reasoning of the author or speaker. In writing and speaking, they enable authors or speakers to strengthen their arguments.

Students are often asked to distinguish between facts and opinions. However, between pure opinion and hard facts lie reasoned judgments in which beliefs are supported by reasons. Instruction in this area needs to be included in all forms of communication in the language arts.

The eight elements of reasoning are introduced to students in **Lesson 8**. Teachers may use the elements to assist in crafting questions for class discussion of literature or questions for probing student thinking. Examples of such questions are given on the Wheel of Reasoning that follows the descriptions below.

The eight elements of reasoning are as follows:

1. **Purpose, Goal, or End View**

    We reason to achieve some objective, to satisfy a desire, to fulfill some need. For example, if the car does not start in the morning, the purpose of my reasoning is to figure out a way to get to work. One source of problems in reasoning is traceable to "defects" at the level of purpose or goal. If our goal itself is unrealistic, contradictory to other goals we have, confused or muddled in some way, then the reasoning we use to achieve it is problematic. If we are clear on the purpose for our writing and speaking, it will help focus the message in a coherent direction. The purpose in our reasoning might be to persuade others. When we read and listen, we should be able to determine the author's or speaker's purpose.

2. **Question at Issue (or Problem to Be Solved)**

    When we attempt to reason something out, there is at least one question at issue or problem to be solved (if not, there is no reasoning required). If we are not clear about what the question or problem is, it is unlikely that we will find a reasonable answer, or one that will serve our purpose. As part of the reasoning process, we should be able to formulate the question to be answered or the issue to be addressed. For example, why won't the car start? or should libraries censor materials that contain objectionable language?

3. **Points of View or Frame of Reference**

    As we take on an issue, we are influenced by our own point of view. For example, parents of young children and librarians might have different points of view on censorship issues. The price of a shirt may seem low to one person while it seems high to another because of a different frame of reference. Any defect in our point of view or frame of reference is a possible source of problems in our reasoning. Our point of view may be too narrow, may not be precise enough, may be unfairly biased, and so forth. By considering multiple points of view, we may sharpen or broaden our thinking. In writing and speaking, we may strengthen our arguments by acknowledging other points of view. In listening and reading, we need to identify the perspective of the speaker or author and understand how it affects the message delivered.

4. **Experiences, Data, Evidence**

When we reason, we must be able to support our point of view with reasons or evidence. Evidence is important in order to distinguish opinions from reasons or to create a reasoned judgment. Evidence and data should support the author's or speaker's point of view and can strengthen an argument. An example is data from surveys or published studies. In reading and listening, we can evaluate the strength of an argument or the validity of a statement by examining the supporting data or evidence. Experiences can also contribute to the data of our reasoning. For example, previous experiences in trying to get a car to start may contribute to the reasoning process that is necessary to resolve the problem.

5. **Concepts and Ideas**

Reasoning requires the understanding and use of concepts and ideas (including definitional terms, principles, rules, or theories). When we read and listen, we can ask ourselves, "What are the key ideas presented?" When we write and speak, we can examine and organize our thoughts around the substance of concepts and ideas. Some examples of concepts are freedom, friendship, and responsibility.

6. **Assumptions**

We need to take some things for granted when we reason. We need to be aware of the assumptions we have made and the assumptions of others. If we make faulty assumptions, this can lead to defects in reasoning. As a writer or speaker we make assumptions about our audience and our message. For example, we might assume that others will share our point of view; or we might assume that the audience is familiar with the First Amendment when we refer to "First Amendment rights." As a reader or listener we should be able to identify the assumptions of the writer or speaker.

7. **Inferences**

Reasoning proceeds by steps called inferences. An inference is a small step of the mind, in which a person concludes that something is so because of something else being so or seeming to be so. The tentative conclusions (inferences) we make depend on what we assume as we attempt to make sense of what is going on around us. For example, we see dark clouds and infer that it is going to rain; or we know the movie starts at 7:00; it is now 6:45; it takes 30 minutes to get to the theater; so we cannot get there on time. Many of our inferences are justified and reasonable, but many are not. We need to distinguish between the raw data of our experiences and our interpretations of those experiences (inferences). Also, the inferences we make are heavily influenced by our point of view and our assumptions.

8. **Implications and Consequences**

When we reason in a certain direction, we need to look at the consequences of that direction. When we argue and support a certain point of view, solid reasoning requires that we consider what the implications are of following that path; what are the consequences of taking the course that we support? When we read or listen to an argument, we need to ask ourselves what follows from that way of thinking. We can also consider consequences of actions that characters in stories take. For example, if I don't do my homework, I will have to stay after school to do it; if I water the lawn, it will not wither in the summer heat.

Adapted from Paul, R. (1992). *Critical thinking: What every person needs to survive in a rapidly changing world*. Sonoma, CA: Foundation for Critical Thinking.

▼ Wheel of Reasoning

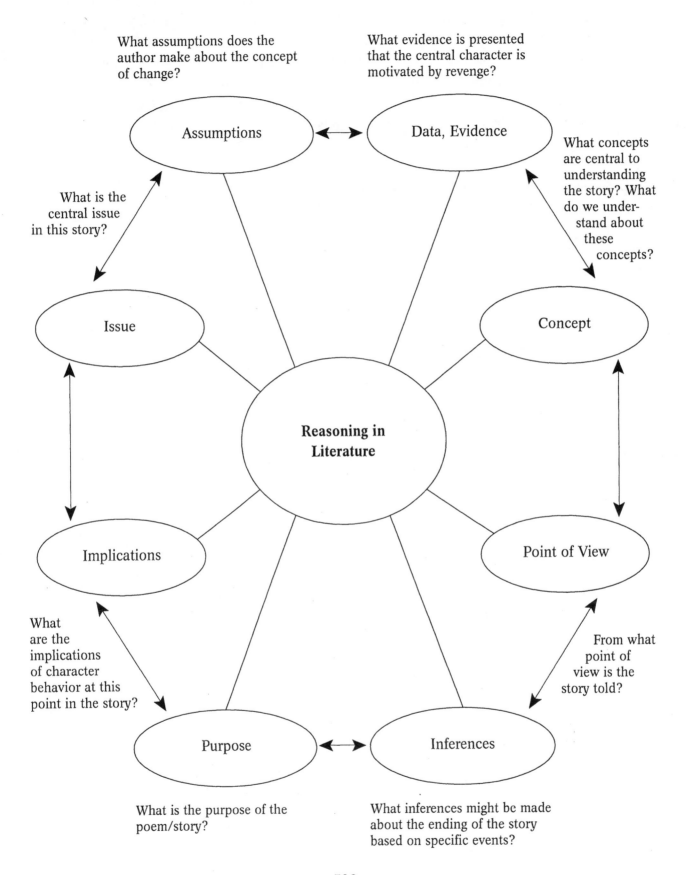

What assumptions does the author make about the concept of change?

What evidence is presented that the central character is motivated by revenge?

Assumptions

Data, Evidence

What concepts are central to understanding the story? What do we understand about these concepts?

What is the central issue in this story?

Issue

Concept

Reasoning in Literature

Implications

Point of View

What are the implications of character behavior at this point in the story?

From what point of view is the story told?

Purpose

Inferences

What is the purpose of the poem/story?

What inferences might be made about the ending of the story based on specific events?

▼ Research Model

The research model provides students with a way to approach an issue of significance and explore it individually and in small groups. Its organization follows major elements of reasoning. Teachers are encouraged to model each stage of this process in class. For specific lessons in teaching the research model, procure a copy of *A Guide to Teaching Research Skills and Strategies in Grades 4–12,* available for purchase from the Center for Gifted Education at the College of William and Mary.

1. **Identify your issue or problem.**

   What is the issue or problem?

   Who are the stakeholders and what are their positions?

   What is *your* position on this issue?

2. **Read about your issue and identify points of view or arguments through information sources.**

   What are my print sources?

   What are my media sources?

   What are my people sources?

   What are my preliminary findings based on a review of existing sources?

3. **Form a set of questions that can be answered by a specific set of data.**

   Examples:

   1. What would be the results of _____?

   2. Who would benefit and by how much?

   3. Who would be harmed and by how much?

   My research questions:

4. **Gather evidence through research techniques such as surveys, interviews, or experiments.**

What survey questions should I ask?

What interview questions should I ask?

What experiments should I do?

5. **Manipulate and transform data so that it can be interpreted.**

How can I summarize what I found?

Should I develop charts, diagrams, or graphs to represent my data?

6. **Draw conclusions and make inferences.**

What do the data mean? How can I interpret what I found out?

How does the data support your original point of view?

How does it support other points of view?

What conclusions do you make about the issue?

7. **Determine implications and consequences.**

What are the consequences of following the point of view that you support?

Do I know enough or are there now new questions to be answered?

8. **Communicate your findings. (Prepare an oral presentation for classmates based on note cards and written report.)**

What are my purpose, issue, and point of view, and how will I explain them?

What data will I use to support my point of view?

How will I conclude my presentation?

SECTION

V

BIBLIOGRAPHIES

This section includes two bibliographies of works used in the unit. The first bibliography lists student readings employed directly in the unit or referenced in extension activities. The second bibliography lists teacher resources.

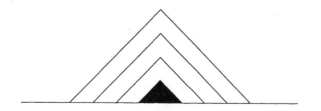

▼ Bibliography of Student Readings

American voices: Prize-winning essays on freedom of speech, censorship and advertising bans. (1987). New York: Philip Morris.

Ashabranner, B. (1984). *Morning star, black sun: The Northern Cheyenne Indians and America's energy crisis.* New York: Dodd, Mead.

Barrie, Sir J. M. (1991). *Peter Pan.* Oxford: Oxford University Press.

Browning, R. (1949). *Poems of Robert Browning.* London: Oxford University Press.

Censorship: For & against. (1971). New York: Hart.

Censorship: Opposing viewpoints. (1990). San Diego, CA: Greenhaven.

Elliot, E. (Ed.). (1991). *American literature: A Prentice Hall anthology.* Englewood, NJ: Prentice Hall.

Frost, R. (1954). *You come too: Favorite poems for young readers.* New York: Holt.

Frost, R. (1982). *A swinger of birches: Poems of Robert Frost.* Owings Mills, MD: Stemmer House.

Hall, H., & Middlemass, R. (1949). The valiant. In Cerf, B. A. and Van Carlnell, H. (Eds.). *Thirty famous one-act plays.* New York: Modern Library.

Hamilton, E. (1932). *The Roman way.* New York: W. W. Norton

Hamilton, E. (1942). *The Greek way.* New York: Modern Library.

Hamilton, E. (1942). *Mythology.* Boston: Little, Brown.

Highwater, J. (1978). *Many smokes, many moons: A chronology of American Indian history through Indian art.* Philadelphia: J. B. Lippincott Company.

Highwater, J. (1983). *Arts of the Indian Americans: Leaves from the sacred tree.* New York: Harper & Row.

Hirschberg, S. (1992). *One world, many cultures.* New York: Macmillan.

Hirschfelder, A. B., & Singer, B. R. (1992). *Rising voices: Writings of young Native Americans.* New York: Scribner's.

Kienzle, N. K. (1981). *Persuade.* [Game]. Colorado Springs, CO: Meriwether/Contemporary Drama.

Martignoni, M. E. (1955). *The illustrated treasury of children's literature.* New York: Grosset and Dunlap.

Mohr, N. (1986). *Going home.* New York: Bantam.

Page, C. H. (Undated). *The chief American poets.* New York: Houghton Mifflin.

Ravitch, D. (1990). *The American reader: Words that moved a nation.* New York: HarperCollins.

Rose, R. (1990). Twelve angry men. In Kaufman, W. I. (Ed). *Great television plays.* New York: Dell.

Soto, G. (1991). *Taking sides.* San Diego, CA: Harcourt Brace Jovanovich.

Tate, E. E. (1987). *The secret of Gumbo Grove.* New York: Franklin Watts.

Taylor, M. (1976). *Roll of thunder, hear my cry.* New York: Dial.

Twain, M. (1996). *The adventures of Tom Sawyer.* New York: Oxford University Press.

Uchida, Y. (1985). *Journey to Topaz* (rev. ed.). Berkeley, CA: Creative Arts Books.

Yep, L. (1975). *Dragonwings.* New York: HarperCollins.

▼ Bibliography of Teacher Resources

American heritage dictionary of the English language. (3rd. ed). (1992). Boston: Houghton-Mifflin.

American voices: Prize-winning essays on freedom of speech, censorship and advertising bans. (1987). New York: Philip Morris.

Appel, A. Jr. (1992). *The art of celebration: Twentieth-century painting, literature, sculpture, photography, and jazz.* New York: Alfred A. Knopf.

Barth, J. L., & Shermis, S. S. (1981). *Teaching social studies to the gifted and talented.* Indianapolis, IN: Indiana State Department of Public Instruction; Lafayette, IN: Purdue University Division of Curriculum. (ED 212118)

Baskin, B. H., & Harris, K. H. (1980). *Books for the gifted child.* New York: Bowker.

Beahm, G. (Ed.). (1993). *War of words: The censorship debate.* Kansas City, MO: Andrews and McMeel.

Bishop, R. S. (1987). Extending multicultural understanding through children's books. In B. E. Cullinan (Ed.), *Children's literature in the reading program* (pp. 60–67). Newark, DE: International Reading Association.

Boyce, L. N. (1997). *A guide to teaching research skills and strategies in grades 4–12.* Williamsburg, VA: Center for Gifted Education.

Bradbury, N. M., & Quinn, A. (1991). *Audiences and intentions: A book of arguments.* (1991). New York: Macmillan.

Burkhalter, N. (1995). A Vygotsky-based curriculum for teaching persuasive writing in the elementary grades. *Language Arts, 72,* 192–196.

Censorship: For & against. (1971). New York: Hart.

Censorship: Opposing viewpoints. (1990). San Diego: Greenhaven.

Chaney, A. L. (1992, June). *Issues in contemporary oral communication instruction.* Paper presented at the Language Arts Summer Institute, College of William and Mary, Williamsburg, VA.

Costa, A. L. (Ed.). (1991). *Developing minds.* (Rev. ed., Vol. 1–2) Alexandria, VA: Association for Supervision and Curriculum Development.

Dallas Museum of Art. (1989). *Ancestral legacy: The African impulse in African-American art.* Dallas, TX: Author.

Doyle, R. P. (1991). *Banned books week '91: Celebrating the freedom to read.* Chicago, IL: American Library Association.

Elliot, E. (Ed.). (1991). *American literature: A Prentice Hall anthology.* Englewood, NJ: Prentice Hall.

Feder, N. (1965). *American Indian art.* New York: Harry N. Abrams.

Frank, M. (1987). *Complete writing lessons for the middle grades.* Nashville, TN: Incentive Publication.

Furst, P. T., & Furst, J. L. (1982). *North American Indian art.* New York: Rizzoli.

Gentile, C. (1992). *Exploring new methods for collecting students' school-based writing: NAEP's 1990 portfolio study.* Washington, DC: U.S. Government Printing Office.

Goodrich, F., & Hackett, A. (1985). *Enjoying literature.* New York: Macmillan.

Haight, A. L. (1978). *Banned books 387 B.C. to 1978 A.D.* New York: Bowker.

Hall, H., & Middlemass, R. (1949). The valiant. In Cerf, B. A., & Van Carlnell, H. (Eds.). *Thirty famous one-act plays.* New York: Modern Library.

Halsted, J. W. (1988). *Guiding gifted readers: From preschool through high school.* Columbus, OH: Ohio Psychology Press.

Halsted, J. W. (1994). *Some of my best friends are books.* Columbus, OH: Ohio Psychology Press.

Hamilton, E. (1932). *The Roman way.* New York: W. W. Norton

Hamilton, E. (1942). *The Greek way.* New York: Modern Library.

Hamilton, E. (1942). *Mythology.* Boston: Little, Brown.

Harris, V. J. (Ed.). (1992). *Teaching multicultural literature in grades K–8.* Norwood, MA: Christopher-Gordon.

Hauser, P., & Nelson, G. A. (1988). *Books for the gifted child, volume 2.* New York: Bowker.

Highwater, J. (1978). *Many smokes, many moons: A chronology of American Indian history through Indian art.* Philadelphia: J. B. Lippincott Company.

Highwater, J. (1983). *Arts of the Indian Americans: Leaves from the sacred tree.* New York: Harper & Row.

Hirschberg, S. (1990). *Strategies of argument.* New York: Macmillan.

Hirschberg, S. (1992). *One world many cultures.* New York: Macmillan.

Kaufer, D. S., Geisler, C. D., & Neuwirth, C. M. (1989). *Arguing from sources.* New York: Harcourt Brace Jovanovich.

Kennedy, C. (1994). Teaching with writing: The state of the art. In Center for Gifted Education (Ed.), *Language Arts Topics Papers.* Williamsburg, VA: Center for Gifted Education, College of William and Mary.

Kennedy, X. J., Kennedy, D. M., & Weinhaus, K. A. (1982). *Knock at a star: A child's introduction to poetry.* Boston: Little, Brown.

Kienzle, N. K. (1981). *Persuade.* [Game]. Colorado Springs, CO: Meriwether/Contemporary Drama.

Koch, K., & Farrell, K. (Eds.). (1985). *Talking to the sun: An illustrated anthology of poems for young people.* New York: Henry Holt.

Langrehr, J. (1988). *Teaching students to think.* Bloomington, IN: National Education Service.

Levine, E. (1989). *I hate English!* New York: Scholastic.

Lipson, G. B., & Romatowski, J. A. (1983). *Ethnic pride.* Carthage, IL: Good Apple.

Lipson, G. C., & Greenberg, B. N. (1981). *Extra! Extra! Read all about it: How to use the newspaper in the classroom.* Carthage, IL: Good Apple.

Lucas, S. E. (1986). *The art of public speaking.* New York: Random House.

Martignoni, M. E. (1955). *The illustrated treasury of children's literature.* New York: Grosset and Dunlap.

Marzano, R. J. (1992). *Cultivating thinking in English*. Urbana, IL: National Council of Teachers of English.

Marzano, R. J., Pickering, D. J., Arrendondo, D. E., Blackburn, G. J., Brandt, R. S., & Moffett, C. A. (1992). *Dimensions of learning: Teacher's manual*. Alexandria, VA: Association for Supervision and Curriculum Development.

Miller, R. K. (1992). *The informed argument: A multidisciplinary reader and guide* (3rd ed.). Fort Worth, TX: Harcourt Brace Jovanovich.

Miller-Lachmann, L. (1992). *Our family, our friends, our world: An annotated guide to significant multicultural books for children and teenagers*. New Providence, NJ: Bowker.

Minn, L. B. (1982). *Teach speech: Oral presentation strategies*. Carthage, IL: Good Apple.

National Assessment Examining Board. (1992). *Exploring new methods for collecting students' school-based writing: NAEP's portfolio study*. Washington, DC: U.S. Government Printing Office.

National Assessment Examining Board. (1992). *Reading framework for the 1992 National Assessment of Educational Progress*. Washington, DC: U.S. Government Printing Office.

National Museum of Women in the Arts. (1987). *Women in the arts*. New York: Harry N. Abrams.

New York Public Library. (1984). *Censorship: 500 years of conflict*. New York: Oxford University Press.

Page, C. H. (Undated). *The chief American poets*. New York: Houghton Mifflin.

Paul, R. (1992). *Critical thinking: What every person needs to survive in a rapidly changing world*. Sonoma, CA: The Foundation for Critical Thinking.

Paul, R., Binker, A. J. A., Jensen, K., & Kreklau, H. (1990). *Critical thinking handbook: 4th–6th grades, a guide for remodeling lesson plans in language arts, social studies, and science*. Rohnert Park, CA: Sonoma State University, Foundation for Critical Thinking.

Plotz, H. (Ed.). (1977). *The gift outright: America to her poets*. New York: Greenwillow.

Polette, N. (1984). *The research book for gifted programs*. O'Fallon, MO: Book Lures.

Public Agenda Foundation. (1987). *Freedom of speech: Where to draw the line*. Dayton, OH: Domestic Policy Association.

Ravitch, D. (1990). *The American reader: Words that moved a nation*. New York: HarperCollins.

Rose, R. (1990). Twelve angry men. In Kaufman, W. I. (Ed). *Great television plays*. New York: Dell.

Rottenberg, A. T. (1991). *Elements of argument: A text and reader* (3rd ed.). Boston: Bedford Books of St. Martin's Press.

Ryan, M. (1987). *So you have to give a speech!* New York: Franklin Watts.

Seiger-Ehrenberg, S. (1985). Concept development. In A. L. Costa (Ed.), *Developing minds: A resource book for teaching thinking*. Alexandria, VA: Association for Supervision and Curriculum Development.

Shrodes, C., Finestone, H., & Shugrue, M. (1992). *The Conscious Reader* (5th ed.). New York: Macmillan.

Soto, G. (1991). *Taking sides*. San Diego, CA: Harcourt Brace Jovanovich.

Stanford, J. A. (1993). *Connections: A multicultural reader for writers*. Mountain View, CA: Mayfield.

Sullivan, C. (Ed.). (1989). *Imaginary gardens: American poetry and art for young people*. New York: Harry N. Abrams.

Sullivan, C. (Ed.) (1991). *Children of promise: African-American literature and art for young people*. New York: Harry N. Abrams.

Sullivan, C. (Ed.) (1994). *Here is my kingdom: Hispanic-American art for young people*. New York: Harry N. Abrams.

Swann, B., & Krupat, A. (Eds.). (1987). *I tell you now: Autobiographical essays by Native American writers*. Lincoln, NE: University of Nebraska Press.

Swicord, B. (1984). Debating with gifted fifth and sixth graders—Telling it like it was, is, and could be. *Gifted Child Quarterly, 28,* 127–129.

Taba, H. (1962). *Curriculum development: Theory and practice*. New York: Harcourt, Brace & World.

Tchudi, S. (1991). *Planning and assessing the curriculum in English language arts*. Alexandria, VA: Association for Supervision and Curriculum Development.

Thompson, M. C. (1990). *Classics in the classroom*. Monroe, NY: Trillium.

Thompson, M. C. (1990–1991). *The word within the word* (vols. 1 & 2). Unionville, NY: Trillium.

Thompson, M. C. (1991). *The magic lens: A spiral tour through the human ideas of grammar*. Unionville, NY: Trillium.

Tiedt, I. M. (1989). *Writing: From topic to evaluation*. Boston: Allyn & Bacon.

Toulmin, S., Rieke, R., & Janik, A. (1979). *An introduction to reasoning*. New York: Macmillan.

UNICEF Ontario Development Education Committee. (1988). *Children's literature: Springboard to understanding the developing world*. Canada: Canadian International Development Agency.

VanTassel-Baska, J. (1992). *Planning effective curriculum for gifted learners*. Denver, CO: Love.

VanTassel-Baska, J., Johnson, D. T., & Boyce, L. N. (Eds.). (1996). *Developing verbal talent*. Boston: Allyn & Bacon.

Vetrone, K. (1986). No need to see. *Gifted Child Today, 9*(2), 41–45.

Whitehead, R. (1968). *Children's literature: Strategies of teaching*. Englewood Cliffs, NJ: Prentice-Hall.

APPENDIX

▼

THE CONCEPT OF CHANGE

This unit is organized around the concept of change and how it functions in literature, writing, speech, and language. As a theme in literature, it is viewed at the level of character growth and development over time and at the levels of social and cultural change which are apparent in literary contexts.

Teachers are encouraged to read the following paper as a prelude to teaching the concept of change. The paper provides a broad-based background in understanding the concept and additional readings for further understanding.

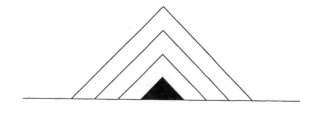

▼ The Concept of Change: Interdisciplinary Inquiry and Meaning

by Linda Neal Boyce

What Is Change?

Because change is a complex concept that inspires fear as well as hope, the idea of change has engaged thinkers throughout the ages and across disciplines. Change is therefore best studied as an interdisciplinary concept for several reasons. First, an understanding of change in one discipline informs the study of change in another discipline and results in important connections. Secondly, an interdisciplinary study of change provides insights into the structure of each discipline. Equally important, the increasing rate of global change resulting in social, political, and environmental upheaval, an information explosion, and a technological revolution creates an urgent need to understand the dynamics of change.

To provide a basis for understanding change as a concept, this paper explores change in several disciplines. While exploring the concepts, it identifies resources for teachers and for students that focus on change. Finally, the paper examines the way the concept of change was applied in the National Language Arts Project for High Ability Learners.

Religion and Philosophy

The *Encyclopedia of Philosophy* (Capek, 1967) and *Encyclopedia of Religion and Ethics* (Hyslop, 1910) provide overviews of change from the perspectives of religion and philosophy. Both sources agree that change is one of the most basic and pervasive features of our experience. Hyslop goes so far as to say that change is difficult to define and that it is easier to discuss the types of change. He identifies four types of change: (1) qualitative change, a change in the qualities or properties of a subject such as chemical reaction; (2) quantitative change which includes expansion, contraction, detrition, and accretion; (3) local change, or a change in the subject's position in space; and (4) formal change, a change of shape. He adds that all changes involve time which is an essential condition of change.

Historically, philosophers and theologians have not always acknowledged the existence of change (Capek, 1967; Hyslop, 1910). Ideas of God, Being, and One that are based on eternal order and perfection of nature regard time and change as illusions of finite experience. Hyslop points out that acknowledging change is crucial to inquiry; that change represents the dynamic as the source of all investigations into causes. He states, "Curiosity regarding causal agency begins with the discovery of change and terminates in explanation" (p. 357). Capek's and Hyslop's essays offer an important backdrop to our understanding of the current controversies, the intense emotion, and the values that surround the concept of change.

Social Studies

In his outline of "Social Studies within a Global Education," Kniep (1989/1991) identifies change as one of the conceptual themes for social studies and asserts, "The process of movement from one state of being to another is a universal aspect of the planet and is an inevitable part of life and living" (p. 121). He lists adaptation, cause and effect, development, evolution, growth, revolution, and time as related concepts. Kniep's comprehensive scope and sequence for social studies includes: (1) essential elements (systems, human values, persistent issues and problems, and global history); (2) conceptual themes (interdependence, change, culture, scarcity, and conflict); (3) phenomenological themes (people, places, and events); and (4) persistent problem themes (peace and security, national/international development, environmental problems, and human rights). Change is both a concept to understand and an agent to consider in all social studies ideas and themes.

In discussing social change, Daniel Chirot (1985) views social change as pervasive. He states that most societies, however, delude themselves into believing that stability prevails and that unchanging norms can be a reality.

Chirot identifies demographic change, technological change, and political change as the most important causes of general social change. In his discussion of how and why critical changes have occurred, Chirot considers three transformations in social structure among the most important:

▼ the technological revolution produced by the adoption of sedentary agriculture

▼ the organizational revolution that accompanied the rise of states

▼ the current "modernization" that encompasses major changes in thought, technology, and politics (p. 761).

He points out that studying current major changes such as the increasing power of the state and the proletarianization of labor helps us understand smaller changes such as those in family structure, local political organizations, types of protest, and work habits. Because change impacts on our lives in large and small ways, we must understand and confront it.

Vogt's (1968) analysis of cultural change echoes Chirot's discussion of social change: "It can now be demonstrated from our accumulated archeological and historical data that a culture is never static, but rather that one of its most fundamental properties is change" (p. 556). Vogt cites three factors that influence change in a given culture:

▼ Any change in the ecological niche as a result of natural environmental changes or the migration of a society as when the Anasazi Indians left Mesa Verde to find new homes and lost their cultural identity in the process

▼ Any contact between two societies with different cultural patterns as when Hispanic and Native American cultures converged in New Mexico

▼ Any evolutionary change occurring within a society such as when a food-gathering society domesticates its plants and animals or incorporates technology to effect lifestyle changes.

In his discussion of cultural adaptation, Carneiro (1968) distinguishes between cultural adaptation (the adjustment of a society to its external and internal conditions) and cultural evolution (change by which a society grows complex and better integrated). Adaptation may include simplification and loss resulting from a deteriorating environment. Thus, adaptation may signal negative as well as positive changes for a cultural group.

History—the social sciences discipline that chronicles change—provides insight into specific changes from a range of perspectives. For instance, resources such as *The Timetables of History* (Grun, 1991) and the *Smithsonian Timelines of the Ancient World* (Scarre, 1993) record changes by significant annual events in the areas of history and politics; literature and theater; religion, philosophy, and learning; the visual arts; music; science and technology; and daily life. These tools allow readers to see at a glance the simultaneous events and significant people involved in changes occurring throughout the world or in a specific area.

Various scholars chronicle ideas about change on an interdisciplinary canvas. Boorstin (1983) focuses on man's need to know and the courage of those who challenged dogma at various times in history. He provides an in-depth look at the causes of change, considering such questions as why the Chinese did not "discover" Europe and America and why the Egyptians and not the Greeks invented the calendar. Tamplin (1991) demonstrates the interrelationship of personal, cultural, and societal change with discussions and illustrations of literature, visual arts, architecture, music, and the performing arts. Petroski (1992) chronicles change and investigates its origins through technology. He argues that shortcomings are the driving force for change and sees inventors as critics who have a compelling urge to tinker with things and to improve them.

Science

Echoing the call for curriculum reform that centers on an in-depth study of broad concepts, Rutherford and Ahlgren (1979) in *Science for All Americans* state:

> Some important themes pervade science, mathematics, and technology and appear over and over again, whether we are looking at an ancient civilization, the human body, or a comet. They are ideas that transcend disciplinary boundaries and prove fruitful in explanation, in theory, in observation, and in design.

Rutherford and Ahlgren proceed to recommend six themes: systems, models, constancy, patterns of change, evolution, and scale. Of the six themes, three of them—constancy, patterns of change, and evolution—focus on change or its inverse. In discussing patterns of change, Rutherford and Ahlgren identify three general categories, all of which have applicability in other disciplines: (1) changes that are steady trends, (2) changes that occur in cycles, and (3) changes that are irregular.

Sher (1993) identifies and discusses four general patterns of change: (1) steady changes: those that occur at a characteristic rate; (2) cyclic changes: those changes that repeat in cycles; (3) random changes: those changes that occur irregularly, unpredictably, and in a way that is mathematically random; and (4) chaotic change: change that appears random and irregular on the surface, but is in fact or principle predictable. She considers the understanding of chaotic change as one of the most exciting developments in recent science.

As in the other disciplines, change in science can be studied as a concept and as a specific application or type of change. For example, our view of the earth over the last 40 years has changed from a static globe model to a dynamic plate tectonics model, affecting our understanding of earthquakes, volcanoes, and other seismic events (NASA, 1988; 1990).

Language—Creative and Changing

S. I. and Alan Hayakawa in *Language in Thought and Action* (1990) state categorically, "Language . . . makes progress possible" (p. 7). They argue that reading and writing make it possible to pool experience and that "cultural and intellectual cooperation is, or should be, the great principle of human life" (p. 8). They then examine the relationships among language, thought, and behavior and how language changes thinking and behavior. For instance, they discuss how judgments stop thought therefore leading to unfounded and dangerous generalizations. They explore the changing meanings of words and point out "no word ever has exactly the same meaning twice" (p. 39). For the Hayakawas, dictionaries are not authoritative statements about words but rather historical records of the meanings of words. Finally, the Hayakawas discuss the paralyzing effects of fear of change and the anger that accompanies it. They propose that the debate around issues facing society should center on specific questions such as "What will be the results?" "Who would benefit, and by how much?" and "Who would be harmed, and to what degree?" rather than questions of "right" or "wrong." They contend that this way of thinking reflects a scientific attitude and harnesses language to accurately "map" social and individual problems, thereby enabling change.

While *Language in Thought and Action* is an eloquent manifesto about the possibilities of language, the anthology *Language Awareness* (Eschholz, Rosa, & Clark, 1982) provides a resource on specific topics. The essays cover the history of language; language in politics and propaganda; the language of advertising; media and language; jargon; names; prejudice and language; taboos and euphemisms; language play; and the responsible use of language. Each essay examines either changes in language or how language changes thinking and action. For example, in her outline of the devices of propaganda that include name calling, generalities, "plain folks" appeal, stroking, personal attacks, guilt or glory by association, bandwagon appeals, faulty cause and effect, false analogy, and testimonials, Cross (1982) examines the manipulative power of language.

The powers of language range from strident manipulation to the quiet heightening of awareness. Response to language involves a change—a change of perspective, a new understanding, an insight in the search for meaning. Coles (1989) speaks of the power of literature to give direction to life and to awaken moral sensibilities. He states, "Novels and stories are renderings of life; they cannot only keep us company, but admonish us, point us in new directions, or give us the courage to stay a given course" (p. 159).

While Coles discusses the impact of literature on private lives, Downs (1978) discusses revolutionary books throughout history in his *Books That Changed the World*. Examining such books as *The Bible*, Machiavelli's *The Prince*, Beecher's *Uncle Tom's Cabin*, Darwin's *Origin of Species*, and Freud's *The Interpretation of Dreams*, Downs attempts to discover and to analyze two categories of writings: works that were direct, immediate instruments in determining the course of events, and works that molded minds over centuries. He concludes that, "Omitting the scientists in the group, for whom these comments are less pertinent, the books [which changed the world] printed since 1500 were written by nonconformists, radicals, fanatics, revolutionists, and agitators" (p. 25).

The reading process which enables readers to search for information and meaning is an active, recursive process that includes choosing a book, reading, discussing from the reader's point of view, listening to another's point of view, reflecting and responding, and re-reading or making a new choice (Bailey, Boyce, VanTassel-Baska, 1990). Effective reading includes revising an interpretation or changing ideas, a step which is mirrored in the writing process and in speaking and listening. Kennedy (1993) sees all of the language processes—reading, writing, speaking, listening, and thinking—as complex, interrelated activities; activities that result in a dynamic, changing discourse.

Censorship reflects the public's acknowledgment and fear of the power of language to change thinking, behavior, and society at large. The debate over censorship and freedom of expression has raged for centuries and ranges from the use of racist and sexist language in literature to the effects of violence on television. Plato, one may remember, argued against allowing children to listen to imaginative stories and banned the poets from his ideal society. The continuing controversy regarding the burning of the American flag is one of several censorship issues widely debated in our society that illustrates the linkage of symbols, language, and freedom of expression (Bradbury and Quinn, 1991).

Telecommunications in a Changing World

Telecommunications has dramatically changed our capacity to access information. Electronic mail, known as e-mail, is a telecommunications system that links computers around the world through telephone lines and satellites. It has created significant changes in scientific and business communities such as: increased flexibility for team members working in various locations across time zones, an end to isolation of researchers around the world, and the restructuring of organizations by eliminating corporate hierarchies (Perry, 1992a). Perry also cites the role of e-mail in the Russian coup of Boris Yeltsin and the use of faxes during the Tiananmen uprising. E-mail and fax machines provided sources of information that were difficult to control and allowed dissenters to communicate with one another and with the outside world (Perry, 1992b).

Video, television, cable, compact discs, and computers and the Internet are transforming not only access to information, but the content of information as well. In a recent *U.S. News and World Report* article John Leo (March 8, 1993) discusses the new standard of television news that blends information and entertainment. He contends that images, story line, and emotional impact are replacing a commitment to evidence, ethics, and truth. In another development, compact discs and computers are combining sound tracks, animation, photography, and print information that replace standard multi-volume encyclopedias and that enable users to combine information in new ways. The Grolier Multimedia Encyclopedia (1994) on CD-ROM for example, supplements its text with features such as animated multimedia maps that show the growth and development of American railroads, the women's suffrage movement, and other topics. This changing information technology demands new standards for the evaluation of information and new consideration of how technology can limit or expand thinking.

The Concept of Change and Language Arts Unit Development

For the purposes of teaching the concept of change for the National Javits Language Arts Project for High Ability Learners, five generalizations about change were drawn from the literature of various disciplines. Table I illustrates those generalizations and their accompanying outcomes. Examples of how the generalizations were addressed in the units through language study, language processes, and literature follow Table I.

Language Study

Throughout the units, word study and vocabulary served as a primary source for studying change. Students constructed vocabulary webs that mapped words by: (1) the definition; (2) a sentence that used the word from the literature being studied; (3) an example of the word; (4) an analysis of the word that identified stems (roots, prefixes, and suffixes), word families, and word history. To build on the verbal talent of high ability learners, resources such as *Sumer is Icumen In: Our Ever-Changing Language* by Greenfeld (1978) and *Oxford Guide to Word Games* by Augarde (1984) were included in the units to encourage students to explore language changes and to play with the possibilities of inventing it themselves.

Each unit included a grammar packet developed by Michael Thompson and based on his work, *The Magic Lens: A Spiral Tour through the Human Ideas of Grammar* (1991). Thompson's packets were designed to help students learn why some ideas are clear and others are confusing; to understand the power of grammar to reveal deep thinking and deep meaning. Implicit in this study was the idea that changing the grammar of a sentence or paragraph meant changing its meaning. Literature selections upon which the units were built and the students' own writing provided the context for studying grammar.

Language Processes

The processes of reading, writing, listening, and speaking were studied as change processes. Literature discussions were based on the premise that each person's interpretation and understanding of meaning would be different from another person's interpretation. Through listening to one another, students were encouraged to seek new meaning and to examine how their interpretations changed during the discussion. In like manner, students studied the writing process as a way to explore ideas and to generate their own thinking and learning. The revision stage of writing emphasized seeking feedback and listening to responses from teachers and peers. Considering another's perspective often led to changes in the understanding of one's own work and to subsequent changes in the structure and clarity of the writing.

Oral communications in these units centered on persuasive speaking and critical listening. Students studied how to change their audience's opinion and actions through argument formulation and strategies of persuasion. As students listened to persuasive speeches, they analyzed the arguments and evaluated their effectiveness. Resources for the speaking and listening components included videotapes of master persuaders such as Franklin D. Roosevelt, Martin Luther King, Jr., and Adolph Hitler that provided students with opportunities to consider the role of persuasion in social and historical

▼ Table I
Generalizations and Outcomes about Change

Generalizations	Outcomes
1. Change is pervasive.	Understand that change permeates our lives and our universe.
2. Change is linked to time.	Illustrate the variability of change based on time.
3. Change may be perceived as systematic or random.	Categorize types of change, given several examples. Demonstrate the change process at work in a piece of literature.
4. Change may represent growth and development or regression and decay.	Interpret change in selected works as progressive or regressive.
5. Change may occur according to natural order or be imposed by individuals or groups.	Analyze social and individual change in a given piece of literature.

contexts. Other resources such as *The American Reader: Words That Moved a Nation* (Ravitch, 1990) documented the persuasive role of oral communications such as orations, Congressional hearings, and songs in the process of change.

Literature

Each of the units was developed around literature selections with vocabulary and language study emerging from the selections. The development of the concept of change also emerged from the literature discussions and activities. Typically each literary piece was examined for evidence of character changes, both physical and psychological, as well as social, political, and economic changes. For instance in "The Power of Light" by I. B. Singer (1962) students discussed the issue of whether characters change themselves or are changed by events outside of their control.

In addition to the literature selections which were discussed with the total group, additional resources embedded in each unit illustrated the generalizations about change and addressed the social, cultural and environmental implications of change. For instance, *Commodore Perry in the Land of the Shogun* (Blumberg, 1985) documents the dramatic social and cultural changes created by Perry's visits to Japan in 1853 and 1854. Illustrated with reproductions of primary sources, the account presents misconceptions, hostilities, and humorous episodes encountered from multiple points of view. Change is palpable while reading the book. A very different book, *Letting Swift River Go* by Yolen (1992) tells of the drowning of a Swift River town for the building of the Quabbin Reservoir, a water supply for Boston and now a wilderness area. The open-ended story alludes to necessary tradeoffs and provides opportunities to discuss changes linked to time as well as the positive and negative aspects of change.

Conclusion

The idea of change crosses all disciplines and offers learners an opportunity to construct a concept that will inform their lives in meaningful ways. Because of the accelerating rate of change in our world, students need to understand the concept and to acquire effective tools for meeting its challenges. Language with its powers of inquiry, persuasion, and critique provides a powerful tool for meeting the challenges of change.

Literature, in particular, offers students and teachers a rich content arena for analyzing change and for considering the issues that surround it. Literature captures the voices, the emotions, and the concerns of thinkers through the ages and across cultures. It demonstrates types of change, responses to change, the causes and agents of change, as well as the effects of change. In a time of dizzying change, literature also offers continuity and a welcomed opportunity for reflection.

▼ References

Augarde, T. (1984). *The Oxford guide to word games.* Oxford: Oxford University Press.

Bailey, J. M., Boyce, L. N., & VanTassel-Baska, J. (1990). The writing, reading, and counseling connection: A framework for serving the gifted. In J. VanTassel-Baska (Ed.), *A practical guide to counseling the gifted in a school setting* (2nd ed.) (pp. 72–89). Reston, VA: The Council for Exceptional Children.

Blumberg, R. (1985). *Commodore Perry in the land of the shogun.* New York: Lothrop.

Boorstin, D. J. (1983). *The Discoverers: A history of man's search to know his world and himself.* New York: Random.

Bradbury, N. M., & Quinn, A. (1991). *Audiences and intentions: A book of arguments.* New York: Macmillan.

Capek, M. (1967). Change. In P. Edwards (Ed.), *The encyclopedia of philosophy* (Vol. 1, pp. 75–79). New York: Macmillan.

Carneiro, R. L. (1968). Cultural adaptation. In D. L. Sills, (Ed.), *International encyclopedia of the social sciences* (Vol. 3, pp. 551–554). New York: Macmillan & The Free Press.

Chirot, D. (1985). Social change. In A. Kuper & J. Kuper (Eds.), *The social science encyclopedia* (pp. 760–763). Boston: Routledge & Kegan Paul.

Coles, R. (1989). *The call of stories: Teaching and the moral imagination.* Boston: Houghton Mifflin.

Cross, D. W. (1982). Propaganda: How not to be bamboozled. In P. Eschholz, A. Rosa, & V. Clark (Eds.), *Language awareness* (pp. 70–81). New York: St. Martin's.

Downs, R. B. (1978). *Books that changed the world* (2nd ed). Chicago: American Library Association.

Eschholz, P., Rosa, A., & Clark, V. (1982). *Language awareness* (3rd ed.). New York: St. Martin's.

Greenfeld, H. (1978). *Sumer is icumen in: Our ever-changing language.* New York: Crown.

Grolier multimedia encyclopedia (1994). Danbury, CT: Grolier.

Grun, B. (1991). *The timetables of history: A horizontal linkage of people and events.* New York: Simon & Schuster.

Hayakawa, S. I., & Hayakawa, A. R. (1990). *Language in thought and action* (5th ed.). Fort Worth, TX: Harcourt Brace Jovanovich.

Hyslop, J. H. (1910). Change. In J. Hastings (Ed.), *Encyclopaedia of religion and ethics* (Vol 3, pp. 357–358). New York: Scribner's.

Kennedy, C. (1993). Teaching with writing: The state of the art. In *Language arts topics papers.* Williamsburg, VA: College of William and Mary, Center for Gifted Education.

Kniep, W. M. (1991). Appendix 3: Social studies within a global education. In W. C. Parker (Ed.), *Renewing the social studies curriculum* (pp. 119–123). Alexandria, VA: Association for Supervision and Curriculum Development. (Reprinted from *Social Education*, 1989, pp. 399–403.)

Leo, J. (1993, March 8). Spicing up the (ho-hum) truth. *U.S. News & World Report, 14*(9), 24.

National Aeronautics and Space Administration. (1988). *Earth system science: A program for global change.* Washington, DC: NASA.

National Aeronautics and Space Administration (1990). *The earth observing system: A mission to planet earth.* Washington, DC: NASA.

Newmann, F. M., & Wehlage, G. G. (1993). Five standards of authentic instruction. *Educational Leadership, 50*(7), 8–12.

Perry, T. S. (1992a, October). E-mail at work. *IEEE Spectrum, 29*(10), 24–28.

Perry, T. S. (1992b, October). Forces for social change. *IEEE Spectrum, 29*(10), 30–32.

Petroski, H. (1992). *The evolution of useful things.* New York: Knopf.

Ravitch, D. (1990). *The American reader: Words that moved a nation.* New York: HarperCollins.

Rutherford, F. J., & Ahlgren, A. (1989). *Science for all Americans: Scientific literacy.* New York: American Association for the Advancement of Science.

Scarre, C. (Ed.). (1993). *Smithsonian timelines of the ancient world: A visual chronology from the origins of life to AD 1500.* New York: Dorling.

Seiger-Ehrenberg, S. (1991). Concept development. In A. L. Costa (Ed.), *Developing minds* (Rev. ed., Vol. 1, pp. 290–294). Alexandria, VA: Association for Supervision and Curriculum Development.

Sher, B. T. (1993). *Guide to science concepts: Developing science curriculum for high ability learners K–8.* Williamsburg, VA: College of William and Mary, School of Education, Center for Gifted Education.

Singer, I. B. (1962). *Stories for children.* New York: Farrar, Straus, Giroux.

Tamplin, R. (Ed.). (1991). *The arts: A history of expression in the 20th century.* New York: Free Press.

Thompson, M. C. (1991). *The magic lens: A spiral tour through the human ideas of grammar.* Unionville, NY: Trillium.

Vogt, E. Z. (1968). Culture Change. In D. L. Sills (Ed.), *International encyclopedia of the social sciences*, Vol. 3 (pp. 554–558). New York: Macmillan & The Free Press.

Yolen, J. (1992). *Letting Swift River go.* Boston: Little, Brown.

Order these outstanding titles by the
CENTER FOR GIFTED EDUCATION

SCIENCE

QTY	TITLE	ISBN	PRICE	TOTAL
	Guide to Teaching a Problem-Based Science Curriculum	0-7872-3328-5	$32.95*	
	Acid, Acid Everywhere	0-7872-2468-5	$32.95*	
	The Chesapeake Bay	0-7872-2518-5	$32.95*	
	Dust Bowl	0-7872-2754-4	$32.95*	
	Electricity City	0-7872-2916-4	$32.95*	
	Hot Rods	0-7872-2813-3	$32.95*	
	No Quick Fix	0-7872-2846-X	$32.95*	
	What a Find!	0-7872-2608-4	$32.95*	

LANGUAGE ARTS

QTY	TITLE	ISBN	PRICE	TOTAL
	Guide to Teaching a Language Arts Curriculum for High-Ability Learners	0-7872-5349-9	$32.95*	
	Autobiographies Teaching Unit	0-7872-5338-3	$28.95*	
	Literature Packets	0-7872-5339-1	$37.00*	
	Journeys and Destinations Teaching Unit	0-7872-5167-4	$28.95*	
	Literature Packets	0-7872-5168-2	$37.00*	
	Literary Reflections Teaching Unit	0-7872-5288-3	$28.95*	
	Literature Packets	0-7872-5289-1	$37.00*	
	The 1940s: A Decade of Change Teaching Unit	0-7872-5344-8	$28.95*	
	Literature Packets	0-7872-5345-6	$37.00*	
	Persuasion Teaching Unit	0-7872-5341-3	$28.95*	
	Literature Packets	0-7872-5342-1	$37.00*	
	Threads of Change in 19th Century American Literature Teaching Unit	0-7872-5347-2	$28.95*	
	Literature Packets	0-7872-5348-0	$37.00*	

Method of payment:

❏ Check enclosed (payable to Kendall/Hunt Publishing Co.)

❏ Charge my credit card:

   ❏ VISA   ❏ Master Card   ❏ AmEx

Credit Card No. _____

Exp. Date _____

Signature _____

Name _____

AL, AZ, CA, CO, FL, GA, IA, IL, IN, KS, KY, LA, MA, MD, MI, MN, NC, NJ, NM, NY, OH, PA, TN, TX, VA, WA, & WI add sales tax.

Add shipping: order total $26-50 = $5; $51-75 = $6; $76-100 = $7; $101-150 - $8; $151 or more = $9

Price is subject to change without notice.   **TOTAL**

Address _____

City/State/ZIP _____

Phone No. (   ) _____

E-mail _____

KENDALL/HUNT PUBLISHING COMPANY
4050 Westmark Drive   P.O. Box 1840   Dubuque, Iowa 52004-1840
A16/mkk   Q2   2005   01

Call (800) 228-0810 • Fax (800) 772-9165
Visit us at www.kendallhunt.com

An overview of the outstanding titles available from the

CENTER FOR GIFTED EDUCATION

SCIENCE

A PROBLEM-BASED LEARNING SYSTEM FROM THE
CENTER FOR GIFTED EDUCATION FOR YOUR K-8 SCIENCE LEARNERS

The Center for Gifted Education has seven curriculum units containing different real-world situations that face today's society, plus a guide to using the curriculum. The units are geared towards different elementary levels, yet can be adapted for use in all levels of K-8.

The goal of each unit is to allow students to analyze several real-world problems, understand the concept of systems, and conduct scientific experiments. These units also allow students to explore various scientific topics and identify meaningful problems for investigation.

Through these units your students experience the work of real science in applying data-handling skills, analyzing information, evaluating results, and learning to communicate their understanding to others.

LANGUAGE ARTS

A LANGUAGE ARTS CURRICULUM FROM THE
CENTER FOR GIFTED EDUCATION FOR YOUR GRADES 2-11

The Center for Gifted Education at the College of William and Mary has developed a series of language arts curriculum units for high-ability learners.

The goals of each unit are to develop students' skills in literature interpretation and analysis, persuasive writing, linguistic competency, and oral communication, as well as to strengthen students' reasoning skills and understanding of the concept of change.

The units engage students in exploring carefully selected, challenging works of literature from various times, cultures, and genres, and encourage students to reflect on the readings through writing and discussion.

The units also provide numerous opportunities for students to explore interdisciplinary connections to language arts and to conduct research around issues relevant to their own lives. A guide to using the curriculum is also available.